I0620705

1689 BAPTIST REFLECTIONS

Vol. 1 | Introduction and Of the Holy Scriptures

STEVEN R. MARTINS

Preface by Andrew Mouck

cántaro
publications

cantaroinstitute.org

1689 Baptist Reflections: Introduction and Of the Holy Scriptures
Published by Cántaro Publications, a publishing imprint of the
Cántaro Institute, Jordan Station, Ontario, Canada

© 2026 by Cántaro Institute. All rights reserved. Except for brief
quotations in critical publications or reviews, no part of
this book may be reproduced in any manner without prior written
consent from the publishers.

Unless otherwise indicated, Scripture quotations are from the ESV®
Bible (The Holy Bible, English Standard Version®). Copyright ©
2001 by Crossway, a publishing ministry of Good News Publishers.
Used by permission. All rights reserved.

For volume pricing, please contact
info@cantaroinstitute.org

Library & Archives Canada
ISBN: 978-1-998711-10-9

Printed in the United States of America

TABLE OF CONTENTS

PREFACE

"...and what you have heard from me in the presence of many witnesses entrust to faithful men, who will be able to teach others also." (2 Tim. 2:2)

THE ABOVE CITED VERSE are Paul's words to his spiritual son in the faith, Timothy. Paul charges Timothy to take the teachings he received and entrust them to faithful men—passing down these truths to future generations of believers. In doing so, he emphasizes the strengthening of the church of Jesus Christ and places a high priority on doctrinal purity and clarity. For generations, Christians have heeded this charge, transmitting the unchanging truths of the faith to the next generation—not by reimagining or reinterpreting essential doctrines, but by drawing upon the wisdom of the saints of old, who were diligent students of

God's Word and guided by the Holy Spirit in articulating their beliefs.

Throughout church history, many rich creeds and confessions have been drafted, blessing and edifying the people of God. Among these, one resource that has proven particularly significant—especially for those within the Reformed Baptistic tradition—is the *1689 Second London Baptist Confession of Faith*.

The *1689 Baptist Reflections* series, which will be compiled and published over time by the Cántaro Institute, began as Martins' study notes during a teaching series on the *Confession* at Sevilla Chapel in St. Catharines, ON, Canada. After experiencing the devotional richness of the *Confession*, it was determined that releasing this series would serve not only individual believers but the broader church. In this first volume, Martins offers a concise, paragraph-by-paragraph exposition of the Introduction and Chapter 1 of the *Confession*, which address both the purpose of the *Confession* and a comprehensive treatment of the doctrine of Holy Scripture.

Beyond the clarity, worshipful tone, and gospel-centeredness with which Martins explains the *Confession*, what stands out is the way in which the theological implications are consistently translated into practical application for the Christian life. This is fitting, as the *Confession* serves "as a faithful summary of what the Scriptures teach," offering abundant Scripture references throughout, and drawing out the imperatives for the reader. Indeed, "All Scripture is breathed out by God and profitable for teaching, for reproof, for correction, and for training in righteousness, that the man of God may be complete, equipped for every good work" (2 Tim. 3:16–17).

At the outset of the *Confession*, the address is made "To the Judicious and Impartial Reader." In this, the authors appeal to a particular kind of reader—one marked by humility and a sincere posture of heart. They presume that the individual who approaches the content of the *Confession*, including its Scriptural proofs, with a genuine desire to know the truth and without bias, will find its articulations of Christian doctrine both accurate and edifying. In the same spirit, if you approach this book—and more broadly, this series—with a desire to trace common Baptistic convictions from Scripture to doctrine, and to consider how such truth transforms the way you live, you will certainly be blessed and strengthened in Christ.

"Now may the God of peace who brought again from the dead our Lord Jesus, the great shepherd of the sheep, by the blood of the eternal covenant, equip you with everything good that you may do his will, working in us that which is pleasing in his sight, through Jesus Christ, to whom be glory forever and ever. Amen" (Heb. 13:20–21).

—**Andrew Mouck**

Chairman, Cántaro Institute
Jordan Station, Ontario, 2025

INTRODUCTION

To the Judicial and Impartial Reader,

Courteous Reader: It is now many years since divers of us (with other sober Christians then living, and walking in the way of the Lord, that we profess) did conceive ourselves to be under a necessity of publishing a Confession, of our Faith, for the information and satisfaction of those that did not thoroughly understand what our principles were, or had entertained prejudices against our profession, by reason of the strange representation of them by some men of note who had taken very wrong measures, and accordingly led others into misapprehension of us and them. And this was first put forth about the year 1643, in the name of seven congregations then gathered in London; since which time divers impressions thereof have been dispersed abroad, and our end proposed in good measure answered, inasmuch as many (and some of those men eminent both for piety and learning) were thereby satisfied that we were no

1

way guilty of those heterodoxies and fundamental errors which had too frequently been charged upon us without ground or occasion given on our part.

And forasmuch as that Confession is not now commonly to be had, and also that many others have since embraced the same truth which is owned therein, it was judged necessary by us to join together in giving a testimony to the world of our firm adhering to those wholesome principles by the publication of this which is now in your hand. And forasmuch as our method and manner of expressing our sentiments in this doth vary from the former (although the substance of this matter is the same), we shall freely impart to you the reason and occasion thereof. One thing that greatly prevailed with us to undertake this work was (not only to give a full account of ourselves to those Christians that differ from us about the subject of baptism, but also) the profit that might from thence arise unto those that have any account of our labors in their instruction and establishment in the great truths of the Gospel, in the clear understanding and steady belief of which our comfortable walking with God, and fruitfulness before him in all our ways, is most nearly con-

cerned; and therefore we did conclude it necessary to express ourselves the more fully and distinctly; and also to fix on such a method as might be most comprehensive of those things we designed to explain our sense and belief of; and finding no defect in this regard in that fixed on by the Assembly, and, after them by those of the congregational way, we did readily conclude it best to retain the same order in our present Confession; and also when we observed that those last mentioned did in their Confessions (for reasons which seemed of weight both to themselves and others) choose not only to express their mind in words concurrent with the former in sense concerning all those articles wherein they were agreed, but also for the most part without any variation of the terms, we did in like manner conclude it best to follow their example in making use of the very same words with them both in these articles (which are very many) wherein our faith and doctrine are the same with theirs; and this we did the more abundantly to manifest our consent with both in all the fundamental articles of the Christian religion, as also with many others whose orthodox Confessions have been published to the world on the behalf of the Protestant in diverse nations and cities. And also to convince all that we have no itch to clog religion with new words, but do readily acquiesce in that form of sound words which hath been, in consent with the Holy Scriptures, used by others before us; hereby declaring, before God, angels, and men, our hearty agreement with them in that wholesome Protestant doctrine which, with so clear evidence of Scriptures, they have asserted. Some things, indeed, are in some places added, some terms omitted, and some few changed; but these alterations are of that nature as that we need not doubt any charge or suspicion of unsoundness in the faith from any of our brethren upon the account of them.

In those things wherein we differ from others we have expressed ourselves with all candor and plainness, that none might entertain jealousy of aught secretly lodged in our breasts that we would not the world should be acquainted with; yet we hope we have also observed those rules of modesty and humility as will render our freedom in this respect inoffensive, even to those whose sentiments are different from ours.

We have also taken care to affix texts of Scripture at the bottom, for the confirmation of each article in our Confession; in which work we have studiously endeavored to select such as are most clear and pertinent for the proof of what is asserted by us; and our earnest desire is that all into whose hands this may come would follow that (never enough commended) example of the noble Bereans, who searched the Scriptures daily that they might find out whether the things preached to them were so or not.

There is one thing more which we sincerely profess and earnestly desire credence in - viz., that contention is most remote from our design in all that we have done in this matter; and we hope that the liberty of an ingenuous unfolding our principles and opening our hearts unto our brethren, with the Scripture grounds of our faith and practice will by none of them be either denied to us, or taken ill from us. Our whole design is accomplished if we may have attained that justice as to be measured in our principles and practice, and the judgment of both by others, according to what we have now published, which the Lord (whose eyes are as a flame of fire) knoweth to be the doctrine which with our hearts we most firmly believe and sincerely endeavor to conform our lives to. And O that, other contentions being laid *asleep, the only care and contention of all upon whom the name of our blessed Redeemer is called might for the future be to walk humbly with their God in the exercise of all love and meekness toward each other, to perfect holiness in the fear of the Lord, each one endeavoring to have his conversation such as becometh the gospel; and also, suitable to his place and capacity, vigorously to promote in others the practice of true religion and undefiled in the sight of God our Father! And that in this backsliding day we might not spend our breath in fruitless complaints of the evils of others, but may every one begin at home, to reform in the first place our own hearts and ways, and then to quicken all that we may have influence upon to the some work, that if the will of God were so, none might deceive themselves by resting in and trusting to a form of godliness without the power of it, and inward experience of the efficacy of those truths that are professed by them.*

And verily there is one spring and cause of the decay of religion in our day which we cannot but touch upon and earnestly urge a redress of, and that is the neglect of the worship of God in families by those to whom the charge and conduct of them is committed. May not the gross ignorance and instability of many, with the profaneness of others, be justly charged upon their parents and masters, who have not trained them up in the way wherein they ought to walk when they were young, but have neglected those frequent and solemn commands which the Lord hath laid upon them, so to catechise and instruct them that their tender years might be seasoned with the knowledge of the truth of God as revealed in the Scriptures; and also by their own omission of prayer and other duties of religion of their families, together with the ill example of their loose conversation, having, inured them first to a neglect and the contempt of all piety and religion? We know this will not excuse the blindness and wickedness of any, but certainly it will fall heavy upon those that have been thus the occasion thereof; they indeed die in their sins, but will not their blood be required of those under whose care they were, who yet permitted them to go on without warning - yea, led them into the paths of destruction? And will not the diligence of Christians with respect to the discharge of these duties in ages past rise up in judgment against and condemn many of those who would be esteemed such now?

> *We shall conclude with our earnest prayer that the God of all grace will pour out those measures of his Holy Spirit upon us, that the profession of truth may be accompanied with the sound belief and diligent practice of it by us, that his name may in all things be glorified through Jesus Christ our Lord. Amen.*

THE OPENING PARAGRAPH of the introduction to the *1689 London Baptist Confession of Faith* asserts that the publication of the *Confession* was a matter of "necessity" for the Baptist leaders who convened in London as early as 1643. But why was it deemed necessary? At the time of its publication, the Christian faith professed by the Lord's faithful was being publicly misrepresented. Moreover, Baptists, as a distinct body within the broader church, were frequently accused of sectarian heresy—an allegation that, in the case of Particular Baptists, was entirely unfounded. While figures such as Matthew Caffyn and Thomas Collier, both associated with the General Baptists, indeed propagated heretical views, the Particular Baptists sought to distinguish themselves from such doctrinal errors.[1] Consequently, the introduction to the *Confession* emphatically declares, "we were in no way guilty of those heterodoxies and fundamental errors which had too frequently been charged upon us without ground or occasion given on our part."[2] Although the precise nature of these historical disputes may no longer be a pressing concern today, the *Confession* remains a vital resource, articulating the biblical foundation of Baptist convictions with enduring theological significance.

Another reason provided by the authors of the *1689 London Baptist Confession of Faith* for the necessity of its publication was that it served as the most comprehensive means of articulating and communicating a summary of what they believed

1. Matthew Caffyn was a Unitarian, he denied the doctrine of the Trinity; Thomas Collier held to a heretical view of the incarnation of Jesus, bordering on the ancient heresy of Arianism. Both Caffyn and Collier, however, held other heretical views which threatened the biblical orthodoxy of the Baptist church.

2. "Introduction", *The 1689 Baptist Confession of Faith*. Accessed November 20, 2023, https://www.the1689confession.com/1689/introduction

according to the revelation of Scripture. This was not limited to doctrinal affirmations alone but also extended to the inward convictions shaped by the work of the Spirit of God. To clarify: while the Holy Scriptures are the inspired Word of God (2 Tim. 3:16–17; 2 Pet. 1:21), the ability to receive them as such requires the regenerative and illuminating work of the Spirit (Ezek. 36:26–27; Jn. 3:5–8). Without this divine work, the heart remains spiritually dead (Eph. 2:1; Col. 2:13), and the eyes remain blind to the truths communicated in God's Word (2 Cor. 4:3).

As one observes from reading the *1689 London Baptist Confession of Faith*, it is not only comprehensive in scope but also systematic in its presentation, enabling readers to return to it repeatedly for diligent study of the Holy Scriptures. However, this does not imply that the *Confession* was ever intended to serve as a substitute for God's Word or to be regarded as equal in authority. While it may communicate infallible truths, it is not itself inspired. Rather, as a faithful summary of biblical doctrine, the *Confession* serves as a valuable tool for studying Scripture, offering extensive Scriptural references for each doctrine it expounds.

Furthermore, the *Confession* does not merely affirm the Holy Scriptures as the ultimate authority for mankind—it presupposes this truth. As stated in its introduction, the Scriptural references provided function as "proof of what is asserted by us," reflecting the example of the Bereans, who, as recorded in Acts 17:10–12, diligently searched the Scriptures after hearing the apostle Paul, "that they might find out whether the things preached to them were so or not."[3]

In addition to the necessity of composing the *1689 London Baptist Confession of Faith*, the introduction also outlines the reasons why it ought to be studied. The fifth paragraph explicitly states its purposes, which include the following:[4]

3. Ibid.
4. Ibid.

11

1. That we would walk humbly with our God;
2. that we would exercise love and meekness toward each other;
3. that we would perfect our holiness out of reverence to the Lord;
4. that the words of our mouth may be the gospel;
5. that we may passionately advance the true religion; and
6. that we may keep the true religion undefiled in the sight of God.

What does the *Confession* mean by the phrase "true religion"? While many today loosely associate the term with works-based righteousness—as reflected in the popular but erroneous slogan "relationship, not religion"—this is not the sense in which the *Confession* employs it. Here, religion is best understood as worship. Thus, we might restate the Confession's stated purpose (5) as "that we may passionately advance true worship." Of course, worship in this context does not refer merely to musical or aesthetic expressions but to worship in its fullest sense—the totality of life lived before God. Worship, as Scripture makes clear, is not confined to liturgical practices but manifests itself in every sphere of the believer's life. The Reformed philosopher H. Evan Runner (1916–2002) aptly captured this reality when he declared, "Life is religion." He was right.[5] Everything we do, think, and say is either an act of vertical worship directed toward God (true worship) or horizontal worship directed toward creation (idolatry). This distinction is evident in the contrast between the church and the world. The life of the church is characterized by the worship of God, while the life of the unbelieving world is marked by idolatrous devotion to creation rather than the Creator (Rom. 1:18–32). More specifically, this idolatry often manifests as the worship of the self.

What I perhaps appreciate most—undoubtedly influenced by my passion for Reformation

5.   For more on this, see *Life is Religion: Essays in Honour of H. Evan Runner*, ed. Henry Vander Goot (Jordan Station, ON.: Paideia Press, 2025).

principles—is the seventh stated purpose of the *Confession*: "to reform in the first place our own hearts and ways."[6] The very notion of *reformation* presupposes that some form of *deformation* has taken place. Indeed, both general and special revelation testify to the tragic reality that our hearts have been deformed by the corrupting influence of sin. The *1689 London Baptist Confession of Faith* thus serves as an instrument of reformation, aligning our hearts—and by extension, our ways—with the teaching of Scripture. Yet, as the authors of the *Confession* recognized, such a reformation is not a mere intellectual or moral endeavor. It can only be realized through the sovereign power and ministry of the Holy Spirit.

The authors of the *1689 London Baptist Confession of Faith* provide one final reason for why we ought to study the *Confession*, as well as why its publication was deemed a necessity. Notably, this reason remains just as relevant in our own time. The penultimate paragraph of the introduction states:

6. "Introduction", *The 1689 Baptist Confession of Faith*.

And verily there is one spring and cause of the decay of religion in our day which we cannot but touch upon and earnestly urge a redress of, and that is the neglect of the worship of God in families by those to whom the charge and conduct of them is committed.[7]

To put it plainly, there is a fundamental reason why our culture has drifted from true worship, why it has degenerated into its present state, and why the church has experienced loss rather than progress in advancing the gospel across every sphere of life. *That reason is the failure of parents to disciple their children.*

In the Old Testament book of *Judges*, the people of God repeatedly fell into cycles of judgment and deliverance. A prevailing reason for their continual descent into judgment was *their failure to instruct the next generation in their faithfulness to God.* Those who had experienced God's deliverance neglected to teach their children to walk in His ways. As a result, each successive generation repeated the sins of

7.   Ibid.

their forefathers, once again falling under the judgment of God. This pattern persisted throughout the book of *Judges*, underscoring a simple yet profound truth: *the lessons learned by one generation were never faithfully passed on to the next.*

The writers of the *1689 London Baptist Confession of Faith* recognized that the church of their time was failing to pass on the faith to the next generation. Tragically, the situation today is far worse. In the seventeenth century, it was the norm for parents to catechize their children, systematically instructing them through a series of questions and answers concerning the truths of Scripture. Today, however, the practice of catechizing has been largely abandoned among Baptists, leaving many parents bewildered as to why their children have not continued in the true faith.

Now, before one raises the doctrine of unconditional election—often invoked to minimize human responsibility—let us be clear: yes, God has elected His people (Eph. 1:4; Acts 13:48; Rom. 8:29), and yes, He has predestined some for salvation (Rom.

8:29; Jn. 15:16; Eph. 1:11). However, God's sovereign work of election, as it unfolds in time and history according to Scripture, *does not negate* human responsibility (2 Cor. 5:10).

The *1689 Confession*, therefore, serves as a vital didactic tool, equipping parents for the discipleship of their children by providing a clear articulation of biblical truth. As believers, we must take up this duty with diligence—faithfully catechizing and instructing our children, whether they be our own or our spiritual children—so that they may be "seasoned with the knowledge of the truth of God as revealed in the Scriptures."

In summary, what is the ultimate hope of studying the *1689 London Baptist Confession of Faith*? Beyond the reasons already outlined, we find a profound expression of this hope in the closing prayer of its introduction:

> We shall conclude with our earnest prayer that the God of all grace will pour out those measures of his Holy Spirit upon us, that the profession of truth may be accompanied with the sound belief and dil-

igent practice of it by us, that his name may in all things be glorified through Jesus Christ our Lord. Amen.[8]

For those seeking a reader's companion to the *1689 London Baptist Confession of Faith*—one that provides both an analytical and theologically rich guide—I highly recommend James M. Renihan's *To the Judicious and Impartial Reader: An Exposition of the 1689 London Baptist Confession of Faith*. Published by Founders Ministries, a Reformed Baptist organization based in Cape Coral, Florida, this work offers a profound exploration of the Confession's theological depth and significance. As Renihan aptly states, "In no way does the *Confession* present dry and dusty theology; rather, it is full of life and vigor."[9] May we likewise find the same vitality and richness as we diligently study the *Confession*.

---

8. Ibid.

9. James M. Renihan, *To the Judicious and Impartial Reader: An Exposition of the 1689 London Baptist Confession of Faith, Baptist Symbolics, Vol. 2* (Cape Coral, FL.: Founders Ministries, 2022), 20.

THE HOLY SCRIPTURES
CH. I, PAR. I

The Holy Scripture is the only sufficient, certain, and infallible rule of all saving knowledge, faith, and obedience,[1] although the light of nature, and the works of creation and providence do so far manifest the goodness, wisdom, and power of God, as to leave men inexcusable; yet they are not sufficient to give that knowledge of God and His will which is necessary unto salvation.[2] Therefore it pleased the Lord at sundry times and in diversified manners to reveal Himself, and to declare (that) His will unto His church;[3] and afterward for the better preserving and propagating of the truth, and for the more sure establishment and comfort of the church against the corruption of the flesh, and the malice of Satan, and of the world, to commit the same wholly unto writing; which makes the Holy Scriptures to be most necessary, those former ways of God's revealing His will unto His people being now completed.[4]

[1] *2 Tim. 3:15–17; Is. 8:20;*
     Luke 16:29,31; Eph. 2:20

[2] *Rom. 1:19-21, 2:14–15; Psalm 19:1-3*

[3] *Heb. 1:1*

[4] *Prov. 22:19-21; Rom. 15:4;*
     2 Pet. 1:19–20

THE OPENING PARAGRAPH of the first chapter of the *1689 London Baptist Confession of Faith* affirms that the Holy Scriptures—namely, the Bible—serves as our sole authority in three essential areas:

(i)   saving knowledge (by which we can know the gospel);

(ii) faith (what it is that we believe); and

(iii) obedience (how we can walk righteously before the presence of God, *Coram Deo*).

The *Confession* supports this claim with four Scripture references in its opening sentence. The *first* of these is 2 Timothy 3:15–17, which states:

[15] and how from childhood you [Timothy] have been acquainted with the sacred writings, which are able to make you wise for salvation through faith in Christ Jesus. [16] All Scripture is breathed out by God and profitable for teaching, for reproof, for correction, and for training in righteousness, [17] that the man of God may be complete, equipped for every good work.

In verse 15, the apostle Paul refers to his spiritual son, Timothy, and how he came to know the salvation that is found through faith in Christ Jesus. This knowledge, Paul explains, was imparted to Timothy through his upbringing in the "sacred writings"—that is, the Word of God. At the time, the New Testament had not yet been fully completed, but the Old Testament, along with the portions of the New Testament that had already been written (e.g., the Gospels), were more than sufficient for Timothy to learn the gospel.

Paul continues in verse 16 by declaring that "all Scripture is breathed out by God." Another way to phrase this is that all Scripture is "inspired by God."

This divine inspiration extends as far back as the first book of the Pentateuch, the book of Genesis. But what does it mean for Scripture to be breathed out or inspired? It means that over the course of thousands of years, the Spirit of God worked through men whom He had appointed, enabling them to write His special revelation.

In this sense, the Bible was written by human hands, making it, in one respect, a human document. This is evident in its diverse literary genres, ranging from historical narrative to poetry, wisdom literature, prophecy, and parables. Yet, the Bible is far more than a mere human document. Behind its human authors stood the Spirit of God who *inspired* the text. Because Scripture is divinely inspired, it is wholly free from error and falsehood in all that it recounts and reveals. As the Reformed theologian R. C. Sproul once said:

> …what Paul is saying when he insists that all of the Scripture has been breathed out by God, he is saying that it's ultimate origin is in Him. It is His word. It is His speech. He is the One who is the source

of these writings. And so when we talk about the doctrine of inspiration, we're talking about the way in which God superintends the writing of sacred Scripture. That God does not just act, and let people respond with their own insight, and their own imagination to set forth their view of what God has done, but that God is working by the Holy Spirit to superintend that record to make sure that the record that is written is His Word.[1]

In truth, there is no other book in all the world quite like the Holy Scriptures. But what purpose do the Scriptures serve? Paul writes that they are "profitable for teaching, for reproof, for correction, and for training in righteousness…" (v. 16). And to what end?

In verse 17, Paul presupposes the sufficiency of Scripture for its intended purpose: "that the man of God may be *complete*, equipped for every good work" (emphasis mine). Here, he affirms that the Scriptures are not merely beneficial but wholly suf-

1. R. C. Sproul, "What does Inspiration mean?", *Ligonier Ministries*. Accessed October, 2022, https://www.ligonier.org/posts/what-does-inspiration-mean-2-timothy-316

ficient to shape and prepare the believer for a life of faithfulness and obedience.

The *second* of the four Scripture references provided is Isaiah 8:20, which states:

> To the teaching and to the testimony! If they will not speak according to this word, it is because they have no dawn.

When we consider this verse within its broader Isaianic context, we see that God is exhorting His people, Israel, to seek guidance from His Word rather than turning to diviners and practitioners of witchcraft. He warns that if anyone claims to offer spiritual insight or direction but does not conform to the Word of God, it is because "they have no dawn"—meaning *they possess no true light within them.* And if they lack the light of God, they are inevitably engulfed in darkness. Through this declaration, God is making a profound statement to His people: His Word is sufficient, His Word is authoritative, and there is no legitimate alternative to His revelation.

The *third* reference provided is Luke 16:29 and 31, drawn from the parable of the rich man and Lazarus. In this true-to-life story (as all parables are), the rich man descends into hell upon his death, while the poor man, Lazarus, is received into Paradise. When the rich man, suffering in torment, pleads with the patriarch Abraham to send someone from the dead to warn his relatives of the judgment to come, Abraham replies that "if they do not listen to Moses and the Prophets, neither will they be convinced if someone should rise from the dead" (paraphrased). Of course, we recognize that such a conversation could not have literally taken place, as there is an unbridgeable separation between hell and Paradise. However, Jesus crafted this parable to convey a fundamental truth: the testimony of the Word of God is wholly *sufficient* for mankind— both for salvation and for righteous living.

Finally, the *fourth* reference provided is Ephesians 2:20, which states:

> …built on the foundation of the apostles and prophets, Christ Jesus himself being the cornerstone…

25

In the preceding verse (v. 19), Paul—writing to the Ephesian church—explains that those who were once outside of Christ were strangers and aliens to God. However, upon being brought into Christ—that is, upon being saved by God's grace—they became fellow citizens of God's kingdom alongside the rest of the elect. Paul is speaking here about the nature of the church, and in doing so, he declares that its foundation consists of "the apostles and the prophets"—a reference to the New and Old Testaments, respectively. Furthermore, he states that Christ Jesus Himself is the cornerstone—meaning that Christ is central to all of Scripture. Remove Christ from the Scriptures, and they cease to be meaningful. Thus, as God's special revelation, the Scriptures serve as the very foundation upon which the church is built.

As we continue our study of Scripture, we grow in our understanding of its significance as "the only sufficient, certain, and infallible rule of all saving knowledge, faith, and obedience…" Yet there is more to consider: the necessity of God's Word.

What do we mean by the necessity of the Word of God? To elaborate: When God created the cosmos—including our world—He revealed His goodness, wisdom, and power. This revelation, known as creational or general revelation, is undeniable. Consider what is revealed in Romans 1:19–21:

> [19] For what can be known about God is plain to them, because God has shown it to them. [20] For his invisible attributes, namely, his eternal power and divine nature, have been clearly perceived, ever since the creation of the world, in the things that have been made. So they are without excuse. [21] For although they knew God, they did not honor him as God or give thanks to him, but they became futile in their thinking, and their foolish hearts were darkened.

As Scripture reveals, though all people possess a knowledge of God (*sensus divinitatis*), they have rejected their Creator because of their sin nature. This is evident in Romans 1:18, where Paul states that the natural man—that is, the man enslaved to sin—suppresses the truth of God in his unrighteousness. Sin is not merely an act of disobedience against God; it has a deeply corrupting influence. It warps the very nature of man, distorting his thinking and leading to a radical reversal—from holiness and righteousness to profanity and sinfulness.

Because of this corruption, God's general revelation is *insufficient* for fallen man. But why is it insufficient? There are two key reasons:

i.   *General revelation does not reveal the way of salvation.* While creation testifies to the fallenness of the world, making it evident that something is fundamentally wrong, it does not reveal how man can be redeemed. Creation itself appears in need of restoration, yet it does not provide the answer to the problem of sin.

ii. *General revelation is misinterpreted due to the noetic effects of sin.* Because of mankind's sin nature, even if the means of salvation were discernible in creation, fallen man would inevitably distort its meaning. Theologians refer to this as the *noetic ef-*

fects of sin—the way sin clouds the mind, leading to flawed reasoning and a corrupt interpretation of reality. Even if man could hypothetically arrive at a correct understanding of God's revelation in creation, his sinful nature would corrupt that interpretation as soon as he attempted to transmit it. Such is the pervasive influence of sin.

For this reason, God has provided His Scriptural revelation—the *only* authoritative and infallible interpretation of His creational revelation. Without it, fallen man would remain in darkness, unable to discern the truth of salvation.

It was necessary, therefore, for God's special revelation to be written for its preservation and advancement. Preservation from what? As the *Confession* rightly states, from the corruption of the flesh (that is, our sin nature), the malice of Satan (who always seeks to destroy what is of God), and the world (the fallen system of man).

Furthermore, it is through God's Scriptural revelation that we come to understand not only our predicament before Him but also the means of our salvation—that is, how we can be saved. Such knowledge is unattainable apart from Scripture. As the *1689 London Baptist Confession of Faith* states, "Therefore it pleased the Lord… to reveal Himself, and to declare His will unto His church." It is important to recognize that God's Scriptural revelation does not replace His creational revelation; rather, the two presuppose and complement one another. Together, they form the *unified* revelation of God. From this revelation, we learn who God is, who we are, why the world is as it is, how we can be made right with Him, and how we ought to live— in other words, what the will of God is for our lives.

Towards the end of the first paragraph, we encounter a truth of significant importance: the Scriptures, from Genesis to Revelation, constitute the complete revelation of God. In other words, the canon is closed, and nothing may be added to or removed from what God has revealed.

This is why we do not affirm the existence of prophets or apostles today in the special, revelatory sense.[2] No one can rightly declare, "Thus saith the Lord…" beyond what is already revealed in Scripture, for God's Word is sufficient. Likewise, no one can speak with the same divine authority as the twelve apostles. The canon is closed. The Word of God is sufficient. As Hebrews 1:1–2 states:

> [1] Long ago, at many times and in many ways, God spoke to our fathers by the prophets, [2] but in these last days he has spoken to us by his Son, whom he appointed the heir of all things, through whom also he created the world.

In light of all this, how might we discern the heart of God in the giving of His Word? In Proverbs 22:19-21, we read the comforting words of a Father that loves and instructs His people:

2. See Kim Riddlebarger, "The Church as God's Prophet", *Ligonier Ministries*. Accessed September 14, 2022, https://www.ligonier.org/learn/devotionals/church-as-gods-prophet/; and "The Apostolic Church", *Ligonier Ministries*. Accessed September 30, 2022, https://www.ligonier.org/learn/devotionals/apostolic-church/.

¹⁹ That your trust may be in the LORD,

I have made them known to you today, even to
you.

²⁰ Have I not written for you thirty sayings
of counsel and knowledge,

²¹ to make you know what is right and true,

that you may give a true answer to those who
sent you?

You may remove the phrase "thirty sayings"
from Proverbs 22:20 and replace it with *"the whole
Scriptures."* God has given us His counsel and
knowledge so that we may know what is right and
true, with the expectation that we would live according to that counsel and knowledge.

Furthermore, Paul explains in Romans 15:4:

For whatever was written in former days was written for our instruction, that through endurance and
through the encouragement of the Scriptures we
might have hope.

And what hope might that be? The hope of a
renewed world through the gospel, a gospel that

saves and applies firstly to our persons, and then to the world.

Finally, I draw our attention to 2 Peter 1:19–20, a passage that not only affirms the enduring relevance of God's Word but also underscores its primary importance for the believer *individually* and for the church as a *whole*:

> [19] And we have the prophetic word more fully confirmed, to which you will do well to pay attention as to a lamp shining in a dark place, until the day dawns and the morning star rises in your hearts, [20] knowing this first of all, that no prophecy of Scripture comes from someone's own interpretation.

I am reminded of the medieval era when Christians were referred to by pagans—most notably by the Muslims of the age—as being "people of the book." It was a respectful designation for the Christians of the age, and I believe that such a name ought to be used for the church today. We ought to be "people of the book"—or, in other words, "people of the Holy Scriptures." Can such a thing be truly said of God's church today?

THE HOLY SCRIPTURES
CH. I, PAR. 2-3

Under the name of Holy Scripture, or the Word of God written, are now contained all the books of the Old and New Testaments, which are these:

OF THE OLD TESTAMENT

Genesis	*2 Kings*
Exodus	*1 Chronicles*
Leviticus	*2 Chronicles*
Numbers	*Ezra*
Deuteronomy	*Nehemiah*
Joshua	*Esther*
Judges	*Job*
Ruth	*Psalms*
1 Samuel	*Proverbs*
2 Samuel	*Ecclesiastes*
1 Kings	*The Song of Solomon*

Isaiah

Jeremiah

Lamentations

Ezekiel

Daniel

Hosea

Joel

Amos

Obadiah

Jonah

Micah

Nahum

Habakkuk

Zephaniah

Haggai

Zechariah

Malachi

OF THE NEW TESTAMENT

Matthew

Mark

Luke

John

Acts

Romans

1 Corinthians

2 Corinthians

Galatians

Ephesians

Philippians

Colossians

1 Thessalonians

2 Thessalonians

1 Timothy

2 Timothy

Titus

Philemon

Hebrews

James

1 Peter

2 Peter

1 John	*Jude*
2 John	*Revelation*
3 John	

All of which are given by the inspiration of God, to be the rule of faith and life.[5]

[5] *2 Tim. 3:16*

BEFORE ELABORATING on the general content of the Bible, the *1689 London Baptist Confession of Faith* references, at the end of the first chapter's second paragraph, the biblical text of 2 Timothy 3:16: "All Scripture is breathed out by God and profitable for teaching, for reproof, for correction, and for training in righteousness."

What does the apostle Paul mean by "breathed out" as he writes this letter to his spiritual son, Timothy? He means *"inspired."* But not inspired in the way one might feel when hearing a masterful piece of music or witnessing an underdog football team defy the odds to score against a stronger opponent. No, Paul is not speaking of mere human inspira-

37

tion. When he declares that all Scripture is inspired, he means that it is the very *breathed-out* Word of God.

Because Scripture is inspired, it is true in every respect, including in its recounting of historical and geographical details. It is also *authoritative*—and being authoritative, it is profitable for "teaching, for reproof, for correction, and for training in righteousness." Whether or not mankind acknowledges it, the Bible remains binding upon all men, for it is the Word *of God*, given to those who bear the image *of God*, in the created world *of God*. Though human hands penned the Scriptures—evident in its diverse literary genres and human languages—its origin is ultimately not found in man but in the Spirit of God. God not only ensured its transcription, but also its preservation and advancement throughout history.

As we reflect on the second paragraph of the first chapter of the *1689 London Baptist Confession of Faith*, we are prompted to ask an essential question: What is the general message of the Word of

God, and how is this message structured throughout its individual books?

I appreciate the way Chris Bruno, Assistant Professor of New Testament and Greek at Bethlehem College & Seminary in Minnesota, articulates this:

> We need to think about the Bible as ultimately a book that points us to the God who made us, the God who invites us to worship him, the God who invites us to be satisfied in him alone. *The unfolding message of the Bible is really a message about God's work to save his people for his glory...*[1]

This summary is helpful for understanding both the place and the relevance of each book within the canon of Scripture. While there is a clear distinction between the Old and New Testaments, they together comprise the *whole counsel of God*, and as demonstrated by the example of Jesus and

1. Chris Bruno, "The One Word That Explains the Whole Message of the Bible", *Crossway.org*. Accessed Oct. 24, 2022, https://www.crossway.org/articles/the-one-word-that-explains-the-whole-message-of-the-bible/ (italicism mine).

the apostles, the New Testament serves to illuminate the Old. To interpret the Old Testament apart from the revelation of the New is to forfeit its full meaning. Unfortunately, many seminary professors instruct their students to study the Old Testament as though it were exclusively a Jewish collection of writings. Yet, from the earliest days of the church, the Old Testament has been rightly regarded as just as much a *Christian* collection of documents as the New Testament—because both proceed from the same God and together manifest doctrinal and historical unity.

We do not deny the Old Testament's Jewish context and authorship, but we reject the notion that its interpretation should be confined to a strictly Judaic framework. Such an approach is not only short-sighted, but also fails to acknowledge the unfolding nature of God's progressive revelation throughout redemptive history.

Altogether, the Bible consists of 66 books—no more and no less. The Old Testament is traditionally organized into five categories:

(i) the Pentateuch (also known as the Books of the Law or the Torah),

(ii) the Historical Writings,

(iii) the Poetic Writings,

(iv) the Major Prophets, and

(v) the Minor Prophets.

Collectively, the Old Testament forms what is known as the Hebrew Bible, often referred to as the *Tanakh*.

To offer a summary of all 66 books would be too extensive for our present purposes. However, by providing examples from the Pentateuch, the New Testament Gospels, and select Pauline epistles, we can begin to discern how each contributes to the unified and central message of the Bible.

Below is a summary of each book within the Old Testament Pentateuch:

The central message of the book of *Genesis* is that God, the Creator, is faithful to His covenant promises. Despite mankind's sin and rebellion, He assures redemption through the promised seed of

41

the woman.

The central message of the book of *Exodus* is that the God who liberates and enters into covenant with His people must be trusted, obeyed, and worshipped. This deliverance foreshadows the greater liberation of mankind from bondage to sin.

The central message of the book of *Leviticus* is that God, being holy, calls His people to be holy. He provides the means of atonement through animal sacrifice, which foreshadows the perfect and final sacrifice by which He sanctifies His people.

The central message of the book of *Numbers* is that the God who saves is also the God who guides and remains present with His people in a fallen world. The journey to the Promised Land prefigures the rich inheritance that awaits the people of God.

The central message of the book of *Deuteronomy* is that God calls His redeemed people to respond with love and covenant loyalty, demonstrated through worship and obedience to His Law, which reflects His just and righteous character.

To include one historical book from the Old Testament:

The central message of the book of *Joshua* is that God is faithful to fulfill what He has promised to His people, and they are called to receive those promises by faith. This foreshadows the greater promises assured to us in the gospel.

Turning now to the New Testament, we also find distinct categories under which its books are organized. These five categories are:

(i)   The Gospels,

(ii) History,

(iii) Pauline Epistles,

(iv) General Epistles, and

(v)   Prophecy.

As we did with the Old Testament, we will now consider a summary of each of the New Testament Gospels, followed by a selection from Paul's letters to the churches:

The central message of the *Gospel of Matthew* is that Jesus, the King of the Jews, has inaugurated the Kingdom of God. He calls His people to follow Him as disciples and commissions them to disciple the nations, participating in His kingdom work.

The central message of the *Gospel of Mark* is that Jesus, the Son of God and Servant King, came, died, and rose again so that we might know Him, confess Him, and serve Him in faithful obedience.

The central message of the *Gospel of Luke* is that Jesus is the Saviour of the world, who through His life, death, and resurrection fulfills all the promises of the Messiah's first coming as foretold in the Old Testament.

The central message of the *Gospel of John* is that Jesus is the eternal Son of God, sent by the Father and revealed to mankind, who, having returned to the Father, has opened the way of salvation to all peoples and nations.

The central message of Paul's letter to the *Romans* is that God is glorified in a unified, missional church, made one by the gospel and humbled under the sovereign grace of God.

The central message of Paul's first letter to the *Corinthians* is that the church is God's holy temple, called to holiness and submission to the Lordship of Christ, dying to the patterns and sins of this present world.

The central message of Paul's letter to the *Galatians* is that the grace of God and the promise of the Holy Spirit are sufficient for both the salvation and sanctification of His people.

Even from this brief selection, we begin to see the common themes woven throughout each book and letter of the Bible. Together, the 66 books of Holy Scripture form a magnificent mosaic, revealing *the glory of God through the salvation of His people and the judgment of the wicked.*

Naturally, this raises an important question: How did we arrive at these 66 books? Why not 67, 78, or some other number, given the existence of various other documents that have circulated throughout history? This is a question of *canonicity*—why were some books recognized as part of the canon while others were not?

The term *canon* comes from the Greek word *kanon*, meaning a measuring rod or standard. In the usage of the church fathers, the term came to refer to an officially recognized list of books. However, before exploring the principles that determined canonicity, it is crucial to clarify a common misconception: The church *did not create* the canon, nor did it determine it by its own authority. Rather, the canon was *discerned, recognized,* and *discovered* as the authoritative Word of God. Put simply: The books of the Bible are not the Word of God because the people of God accepted them; rather, the people of God accepted them because they are the Word of God. It is God, not man, who gives authority to the Scriptures.[2]

Now, what principles do we find in the *discerning* of the Old and New Testament canon? There were, at minimum, six principles:

2.   The reader would do well to pick up a copy of F. F. Bruce's *The Canon of Scripture* (USA: IVP Academic, 2008).

1. **Was the book written by a prophet or apostle of God?** If so, then it was the Word of God.

2. **Was the writer confirmed by acts of God?** Moses, for example, performed miracles before Pharaoh, as did other prophets and later apostles.

3. **Did the book communicate the truth about God?** If it was found contrary to the rest of Scripture, then it could not form part of the canon.

4. **Does it come with the life-changing power of God?** If it is the Word of God, then its presence must exhibit God's transforming power in those who hear, repent, and believe.

5. **Was it accepted by the people of God?** That is to say, did the people receive it, collect it, read it, and use it as the Word of God?

6. The sixth principle concerns those documents that were, for example, not written

by a prophet or apostle, such as the *Gospel of Luke* and the *Book of Acts*. Both of those were written by the Gentile, Luke, who was just as much a historian as he was a physician. This sixth principle is **if the book had apostolic approval.**

In the era of the early church, the need to compile and rightly recognize the canonical books became increasingly urgent. As the truth of God was proclaimed, counterfeits and heresies soon followed—a pattern we see throughout history (for the antithesis always follows after the proclamation of the thesis). One particularly notorious heretic, Marcion (c. AD 140), developed his own version of the canon, which was radically different from that recognized by the church at large.

Marcion's canon was not only anti-Semitic but also contained Gnostic elements, pitting the God of the Old Testament against the God of the New Testament. This was a gross perversion of Scripture. And because his attempt was neither the first nor the last, it became necessary for the church to formally *recognize* the canon.

This recognition is evident in the writings of the early church fathers, such as Athanasius, who in his writings listed the 27 books of the New Testament canon. Others, including Jerome, Augustine, Polycarp, and Justin Martyr, also affirmed the authoritative books of Scripture. Though we could explore the role of the early church councils and the patristic tradition further, it is a study best left for another occasion. For now, it suffices to say that there is ample textual evidence that the church clearly understood what was canonical and what was not.

Having answered the question of how we arrived at the 66 books, we must now turn to another: What about those other books that were highly regarded by early Jewish and Christian communities yet were not included in the canon?

To address this, we turn to the third paragraph of the *Confession*, which naturally follows from the second for two key reasons: (i) Their connection within the *Confession* itself, and (ii) Their relevance to this follow-up question on canonicity.

The third paragraph states as follows:

The books commonly called Apocrypha, not being of divine inspiration, are no part of the canon or rule of the Scripture, and, therefore, are of no authority to the church of God, nor to be any otherwise approved or made use of than other human writings. [6]

[6]   *Luke 24:27,44; Rom. 3:2*

There are two primary sets of apocryphal writings:

(i) the Old Testament Apocrypha, and

(ii) the New Testament Apocrypha.

Among the Old Testament Apocrypha are books such as *Tobit*, *Judith*, *The Wisdom of Solomon*, and *First* and *Second Maccabees*, among others. In total, there are approximately fifteen such books, many of which appear in the Septuagint—the Greek translation of the Old Testament.

Among the New Testament Apocrypha are writings such as the *Epistle of Pseudo-Barnabas*, the

Epistle to the Corinthians (by Clement), the *Apocalypse of Peter*, and the *Epistle of Polycarp to the Philippians*, to name only a few. In fact, the number of apocryphal texts associated with the New Testament era is vast.

While some of these writings may be of value for historical or cultural studies, they are not to be regarded as canonical. For example, *First* and *Second Maccabees* offer important insight into the intertestamental period—the span of time between the Old and New Testaments—but they are not inspired, and therefore should not be treated differently than other historical writings from antiquity.

Why, then, were these books not considered part of the canon? For the following reasons:

1. Most of the apocryphal writings only experienced a temporary or local recognition, they were never universally recognized;

2. Most of them were appendages to various manuscripts, or mentioned in tables of contents, but never treated as canonical;

3. Not a single legitimate church council included them as inspired books of the Old and/or New Testament;

4. Many of them contained content that contradicted canonical writings, and shows signs of doctrinal compromise with surrounding heretical elements.

The *Confession* references three Scripture passages to support its articulation of the rejection of the Apocrypha.

The first is Luke 24:27, which reads:

And beginning with Moses and all the Prophets, he interpreted to them in all the Scriptures the things concerning himself.

Second, Luke 24:44, which reads:

Then he said to them, "These are my words that I spoke to you while I was still with you, that everything written about me in the Law of Moses and the Prophets and the Psalms must be fulfilled."

In both instances, Jesus affirms the canonicity, inspiration, and authority of the Old Testament Scriptures, which were well recognized by the Jewish community of His day. Importantly, the Jews referred to the Old Testament apocryphal writings as the "Apocrypha," indicating that these books were not regarded as canonical. As such, there would have been no controversy surrounding Jesus' claims.

The third passage referenced by the *Confession* is Romans 3:2, which reads:

> Much in every way. To begin with, the Jews were entrusted with the oracles of God.

The apostle Paul affirms what Jesus affirmed, and so we find agreement as to what is Scriptural, as to what is *canonical*.

What about the New Testament canon? Does the New Testament say anything about that? While there are several general and contextualized passages that we could refer to, we have to understand that the New Testament was still being written in the first century. Thus, for the support of the New Testament canon, it is helpful to consult the church fathers, of whom it is said that the entirety of the New Testament could be reconstructed from their numerous citations in their writings. There was little doubt as to what was canon, and that was ultimately the work of the Spirit of God working providentially through the church and in history. In truth, the composition of Holy Scripture, from beginning to end, from Genesis to Revelation, is a work of God.

THE HOLY SCRIPTURES
CH. I, PAR. 4

*The authority of the Holy Scripture, for which it
ought to be believed, depends not upon the testimony of any man or church, but wholly upon God
(who is truth itself), the author thereof; therefore
it is to be received because it is the Word of God.*[7]

[7]   *2 Pet. 1:19–21; 2 Tim. 3:16; 1 Thess. 2:13;
    1 John 5:9*

O**VER THE YEARS,** during my preparation
for ministry, I benefited greatly from the
recorded lectures of Greg L. Bahnsen,
a remarkable teacher of biblical apologetics and
worldview. In one of his lectures, Bahnsen made
a bold and thought-provoking claim regarding
the authority of Holy Scripture. He asserted that,
when compared to the so-called "holy books" of the
world's major religions, the Bible is the only one

that self-attests to being the inspired Word of God.

This claim is true when you consider the content of the Qur'an, the Bhagavad-Gita, or the Pali Canon. In terms of self-testimony, the Bible stands alone, elevated above all others. And what are we to do with such a claim? We are called to put it to the test, to evaluate whether this self-attestation holds up to scrutiny—whether it is logically consistent. How do we do that? By examining the text to determine: whether it is internally harmonious and free from contradiction (which, to this day, it has proven to be—and will continue to be), and whether it corresponds with reality—in other words, whether it accurately describes the world as we know and experience it. If we can truly make sense of the world through the lens of Scripture, then we can confidently affirm its claim to be the authoritative Word of God.

Where in the Bible do we find its claim of authority? The *1689 London Baptist Confession of Faith* offers several biblical references in support of this claim. We begin with the first one cited in the fourth paragraph of the first chapter, namely 2 Peter 1:19–21.

This is what the apostle Peter wrote:

> [19] And we have the prophetic word more fully confirmed, to which you will do well to pay attention as to a lamp shining in a dark place, until the day dawns and the morning star rises in your hearts, [20] knowing this first of all, that no prophecy of Scripture comes from someone's own interpretation. [21] For no prophecy was ever produced by the will of man, but men spoke from God as they were carried along by the Holy Spirit.

Consider what Peter first writes here in verse 19: "we have the prophetic word more fully confirmed." What does that mean? That the Scriptures—those already in their possession—had demonstrated themselves to be internally consistent, without contradiction, and in correspondence with real historical events. The Scriptures, in other words, dealt with reality, not fantasy. And since the prophetic word was more fully confirmed, we are to adhere to it like a light guiding us in the dark.

Have you ever tried to walk in the dark—without any light? In the dark, you cannot see anything. And if you were to attempt to move in any particular direction, you might walk into a wall, a table, or worse—into oncoming traffic. The truth is, you need light in order to see.

Peter tells us that the Bible is our light. If we are to walk the right path, to live and function rightly, we need the Word of God. Without it, we are left grasping in the dark, unsure of where we are or what we are doing. To put it another way: to live without the Bible is to live without eyes. We need the Bible to see clearly.

And for how long do we need His Word? Until the morning star rises in our hearts—that is, until Christ returns, and we are raised in glory with resurrected bodies, to dwell forever in the new heavens and the new earth. Until that day, we need the Word of God.

What else does Peter say? In verse 20, he writes that no prophecy of Scripture comes from someone's own interpretation. What does this mean? He explains in verse 21: nothing taught in Scripture is of human invention. Here, we are referring to doctrine, not literary form or grammatical structure. No teaching of Scripture originated from a mystic visionary or philosopher with a novel idea. Instead, "men spoke from God as they were carried along by the Holy Spirit." All of Scripture is inspired by God All of Scripture is the product of the Holy Spirit. All of Scripture is the written revelation of God. Therefore, it is authoritative and binding upon all men.

The next passage cited by the *1689 Baptist Confession* is 2 Timothy 3:16—a verse we have previously considered. It comes from what is believed to be Paul's final letter to his spiritual son Timothy, written shortly before his martyrdom. Paul writes:

> All Scripture is breathed out by God and profitable for teaching, for reproof, for correction, and for training in righteousness...

The *1689 Baptist Confession* also cites 1 Thessalonians 2:13, which states:

And we also thank God constantly for this, that when you received the word of God, which you heard from us, you accepted it not as the word of men but as what it really is, the word of God, which is at work in you believers.

Here we find the apostle Paul writing to the church in Thessalonica. He notes that when they "heard" the gospel—when they received the teachings of Paul, which consisted of both Old and New Testament revelation (nothing beyond what we hold in our hands today)—they did not receive it as "the word of men." In other words, they did not treat this message as they did the teachings of the various Greek schools of thought. It was not received as theory, speculation, or mythology. They received it as the Word of God, elevating it far above any human invention.

Perhaps Socrates, Plato, Aristotle, and other philosophers had some wisdom to impart, but their teachings were foolishness when compared to the authoritative revelation of God. The Scriptures became, for the Thessalonians, the final authority.

And although the canon had not yet been completed, what they had already received was recognized as inspired and authoritative.

Moreover, to confirm that the Word was truly the Word of God, Paul testifies that it had already begun to work within them, transforming their lives. Why? Because "the Word of God is living and active" (Heb. 4:12).

The fourth passage cited by the *Confession* is 1 John 5:9, which states:

> If we receive the testimony of men, the testimony of God is greater, for this is the testimony of God that he has borne concerning his Son.

In his first epistle, the apostle John writes that those who have received the testimony of God— that is, the Word of God—have elevated it far above the testimony of men. In other words, no matter what man may produce in his attempts to interpret reality, it can never supplant the Word of God as the ultimate authority.

Does this mean we must dismiss the sciences? Are we to reject the observational findings of biology, chemistry, physics, or astronomy? Certainly not. In fact, far from suppressing the sciences, Scripture has historically inspired and encouraged scientific inquiry and progress.

So how should we understand the implications of John's statement? In its immediate context, John is addressing any testimony that calls into question God's revelation of the Son. However, Scripture often carries multiple layers of meaning—intended not merely by the human author, but by the Spirit of God. In this case, one of those deeper implications is that the Word of God is the chief authority for *all* knowledge.

This is not to suggest that the Bible functions as a textbook on surgery, nuclear fission, or architecture—such a view would be reductive and misguided. Rather, it means that Scripture provides the foundational framework and necessary parameters for interpreting and understanding the world rightly. The findings of the sciences, when rightly understood, are to be seen under the light of God's special revelation.

We need to take note that Scripture was given as the *only* authoritative interpretation of reality. In other words, God's special revelation is the *only* authoritative interpretation of God's general (creational) revelation. The *necessity* of special revelation arises, in part, because of the *noetic* effects of sin—that is, the way sin has impaired human reason and understanding. It is also necessary because general revelation does not reveal the means by which creation can be *redeemed*.

When it comes to interpreting reality, this truth concerning the noetic effects of sin and the necessity for an authoritative and definitive interpretation of creational revelation should not come as a surprise to us. Take, for instance, Charles Darwin's (1809–1882) theory of evolution, which has increasingly shown signs of public collapse. While neo-Darwinism remains widely accepted in our current cultural moment, it is by no means an unassailable fortress. As Gordon Wilson, Senior Fellow of Natural History at New Saint Andrews College, observes:

> Why are brilliant and logical scientists not reasonable on the question of the ultimate cause of the unity, diversity, and complexity of life on Earth? We wrongly think that an accurate view of life's origins can be deduced by science and logic alone apart from faith and humble submission to God's Word. Without the light of God's Word, unbelievers have built up an edifice, a theory of life's origins known as Darwinian Evolution, which they believe is an impregnable fortress. In our Darwin-dominated society, blind chance, mutation, and natural selection have received most of the glory for the unity, diversity, and complexity of life on Earth. It's about time this philosophy is seen for what it is: *a sandcastle on the beach, in the face of the rising tide.*[1]

In affirmation of Wilson's assessment, the gross lack of historical evidence for transitional lifeforms in the fossil record has left (neo-)Dar-

---

1.   Gordon Wilson, *Darwin's Sandcastle: Evolution's Failure in the Light of Scripture and the Scientific Evidence* (USA: Roman Roads Press, 2023), back cover, italicism mine.

winists in utter disarray.

Moreover, the fact that genetic mutations have consistently resulted in the *loss* of genetic information rather than its *increase* directly contradicts Darwin's foundational theory on the origin of species.

The only reason Darwinism has remained culturally and intellectually relevant is because the unbelieving world is desperate for any framework that can serve as a counterargument to the existence of God. This is consistent with Romans 1:18, which tells us that the natural (unregenerate) man suppresses the truth of God in unrighteousness.

What is surprising, however, is how many Christians have attempted to *synthesize* Darwinian evolution with the Christian worldview. And this raises the question: How did such a synthesis emerge in the first place?

The answer lies in this: many of these synthesists have elevated the sciences to an equal or even greater level of authority than Holy Scripture. In doing so, they have exalted the mind of man above the mind of God. To borrow the language of the apostle John, this is to receive "the testimony of men as greater than the testimony of God."

It would be disingenuous to claim that the church has always remained faithful in guarding the authority of God's Word. It has not. Throughout history, there have been moments when the church has elevated autonomous natural reason to the level of, or even above, Scripture. One notable example is the rise of medieval Scholasticism, in which Thomas Aquinas, the 13th-century theologian and philosopher, elevated the writings of Greek natural philosophers to the same level of authority as the teachings of Scripture. On one side stood natural reason, and on the other, sacred grace. This dualistic framework, known as the Scholastic ground-motive of Nature and Grace, has had profound and damaging consequences for Christian thinking and living.

While a fuller discussion extends beyond the scope of this study, those who wish to explore this issue further would benefit greatly from reading Herman Dooyeweerd's *The Roots of Western Culture* and H. Evan Runner's *The Relation of the Bible to*

Learning, which examine the structure of Thesis, Antithesis, and Synthesis, as well as the competing religious ground-motives that have shaped the intellectual history of the West.[2]

Thus far, we have considered the self-witness of Scripture concerning its authority and inspiration. There remains one final point to exposit from the fourth paragraph of the first chapter in the *Confession*—specifically, the phrase: "God (who is truth itself)."

This concluding point presents the chief reason why we ought to believe the Holy Scriptures. If we have established that Holy Scripture is the Word of God, by virtue of its divine inspiration, we must now ask: Why can God Himself be trusted? Why should He be believed?

---

2.   Herman Dooyeweerd, *The Roots of Western Culture: Pagan, Secular, and Christian Options* (Jordan Station, ON.: Paideia Press, 2012); H. Evan Runner, *The Relation of the Bible to Learning: The Unionville Lectures* (Jordan Station, ON.: Paideia Press, 2023).

In John 14:6, Jesus declared, "I am the way, and the truth, and the life. No one comes to the Father except through me." We recognize here a clear claim of exclusivity: no one can come to God the Father apart from God the Son, and no one can receive salvation apart from Christ. However, I want to draw our attention to one of the three claims Jesus makes in this verse—the claim: "I am the truth." Just as the *Confession* affirms that "God is truth itself," so too does Jesus' statement point us to one of the many attributes of God's being.

There are generally two categories of divine attributes: *non-moral* and *moral*. For example, the eternality of God is a non-moral attribute, whereas the righteousness of God is a moral attribute. To say that God is truth is to affirm that truth flows naturally and necessarily from His very nature. God does not merely possess truth; He is the truth. He is the standard by which all truth is measured. Both the Old and New Testaments deepen our understanding of this reality through their respective terms for truth:

- In Hebrew, the word is *'emet*, meaning firm, stable, and faithful. God is thus firm, unchanging, and trustworthy—truth that endures.

- In Greek, the word is *alētheia*, meaning truthful, upright, and without deceit. God is therefore honest, reliable, and entirely without falsehood—absolute truth that can be depended upon.

Consequently, His Word must be true, for God Himself is truth.

In conclusion, Holy Scripture is the guiding light for man's life. It is God's Word to you and me, and if man neglects to read it, his soul will go hungry—and there is nothing in this world that can satisfy that hunger.

For this reason, Jesus refers to the Word of God as our daily bread (Matt. 6:11–15). Do you want to know God? Then study His Word. Do you want to know how to speak with God? Then read His Word. Do you want to know how to live for God? Then live His Word.

What kind of church will we be? A church that loves the Word—or a church that barely reads it?

As Al Mohler once said:

> In the end, the church will either declare the truth of God's Word, or it will find a way to run away from it.[3]

What place does the Word of God occupy in your life? If we hope to be faithful to our Lord Jesus Christ, it must be our *ultimate* authority for all thinking and living.

---

3.   R. Albert Mohler, Jr. *We Cannot Be Silent* (Nashville, TN.: Thomas Nelson, 2015), 117.

THE HOLY SCRIPTURES
CH. I, PAR. 5

We may be moved and induced by the testimony of the church of God to a high and reverent esteem of the Holy Scriptures; and the heavenliness of the matter, the efficacy of the doctrine, and the majesty of the style, the consent of all the parts, the scope of the whole (which is to give all glory to God), the full discovery it makes of the only way of man's salvation, and many other incomparable excellencies, and entire perfections thereof, are arguments whereby it does abundantly evidence itself to be the Word of God; yet notwithstanding, our full persuasion and assurance of the infallible truth, and divine authority thereof, is from the inward work of the Holy Spirit bearing witness by and with the Word in our hearts.[8]

[8] *John 16:13-14; 1 Cor. 2:10-12; 1 John 2:20, 27*

WHAT CAN WE LEARN from the opening phrase: "We may be moved and induced by the testimony of the church of God to a high and reverent esteem of the Holy Scriptures"? We learn that the church—the body of Christ, the community of believers—is to uphold a deep and reverent regard for the Bible as the very Word of God.

When I look back on my own life and consider how I came to develop a love and passion for the Word of God, I can clearly discern how that affection was cultivated. It was the result of the Word being faithfully preached from the pulpit. It was the result of the Word being taught in small group Bible studies. It was the result of brothers and sisters in Christ pointing me to Scripture for wisdom in daily living. Of course, none of these means would have accomplished anything apart from the Spirit of God first working in my heart. Yet, it was precisely through these means that the Spirit cultivated within me a deep and enduring love for the Word.

The true church of God recognizes the inspiration of the Word, and accordingly elevates it to its rightful place as God's authoritative revelation to all people. That said, it is important to clarify that, as Christians, we *do not* idolatrize the Word.

The Bible we hold in our hands is indeed from God—written by human hands under the inspiration of the Holy Spirit—*but it is not God Himself.* We are not like the Sikhs, who venerate their holy book as sacred in and of itself, nor like the Muslims, who treat the Qur'an with the same reverence they show to Allah.

There is a necessary distinction between God and the means by which He has chosen to reveal Himself. The Scriptures are God-breathed, but they are not divine in substance; they are composed of created materials—ink, paper, and binding. What is inspired is the *message*, not the physical medium.

I once had a friend—we'll call him Marco—who was exceptionally zealous about how the Bible was handled. His zeal stemmed from a deep reverence for God, but it was a zeal not tempered by discernment. If someone placed a Bible in the trunk of a car, in a suitcase, or on a chair, Marco would be offended. To him, the Bible had to be set apart physically—almost placed on a pedestal.

While Marco's reverence could be admired in one sense, it risked veering into a kind of Pharisaism. In what way? In that it gave greater attention to the physical form of the Bible than to the message it contains. There are many today who similarly idolize the text—treating the Bible as though it were an extension of God's being—while failing to live in accordance with its divinely inspired truth.

As Christians, we must ensure that our worship is not directed at the text itself, but at the God who reveals Himself through the text. Our reverence for Scripture should always lead us to submission to its message, and ultimately, to the worship of the triune God who speaks through it.

The next phrase states: "and the heavenliness of the matter". This affirms that we recognize the Word as inspired—as the breathed-out Word of God. It is not the product of human invention, not the result of philosophical reflection, and not the output of the fallen human mind. Its origin is in the Spirit of God, and thus the perspective it provides is one from a heavenly vantage point.

Did the human authors have their own intentions in writing? Yes, of course they did. Consider the apostle Paul and his pastoral and theological aims in writing to the churches in Rome, Ephesus, or Corinth. There is certainly a *human aspect* to the Scriptures, as they were penned by men of God. Yet all their writing was subject to the *guidance of the Spirit* and governed by the *sovereign will of God*.

The next phrase in this fifth paragraph reads: "the efficacy of the doctrine." This means that what Holy Scripture reveals and teaches is true.

What Scripture reveals about the nature of God is true.

What it reveals about the nature of man is true.

What it reveals about the state of the world is true.

We know the doctrine of Scripture to be true because it is logically coherent, internally consistent, and it corresponds with the world we see and experience.

The Bible is not a compilation of fairy tales or mythological constructs. It is composed with serious intent, significant detail, and cultural and historical awareness. The historical figures mentioned in Scripture, for example, can often be correlated with findings from the ancient world. The events described within its narrative framework can frequently be corroborated by records from other ancient civilizations. Much could be said about the trustworthiness of the Word of God as it relates to everything it reveals. The truth is, if it were not for Scripture, we would have no certainty about what we are to believe. And this is because the influence of sin on the human mind (the *noetic* effects) would distort all efforts to arrive at sound doctrine. It was, therefore, necessary for God to provide us with true doctrine.

The next phrase reads: "and the majesty of the style." This refers to the excellence of Scripture's literary composition, particularly its employment of sophisticated literary devices.

One such example is the use of *chiasmus*—a rhetorical structure in which words or concepts are repeated in reverse order to emphasize key truths.

Consider Genesis 9:6: "Whoever sheds the blood of man, by man shall his blood be shed, for God made man in his own image." This is a clear instance of chiasmus, where the mirrored structure draws attention to the theological weight of the *imago Dei* as the foundation for justice.

Another example appears in Matthew 19:30: "But many who are first will be last, and the last first." This stylistic symmetry captures and reinforces a profound moral teaching through elegant brevity.

Another literary technique is *acrostic*—a device found in Old Testament poetry in which successive units of a poem begin with the consecutive letters of the Hebrew alphabet. This, admittedly, can only be observed in the original Hebrew text.

There is also the technique of *hyperbole*—the use of deliberate exaggeration for emphasis or rhetorical effect.

For example, 2 Chronicles 1:15 states: "And the king made silver and gold as common in Jerusalem as stone, and he made cedar as plentiful as the sycamore of the Shephelah."

Or consider Mark 9:43: "And if your hand causes you to sin, cut it off. It is better for you to enter life crippled than with two hands to go to hell, to the unquenchable fire."

We could spend hours upon hours examining the literary features of the Word—the excellency of its style and the skill with which these elements are employed—but what I have shared will suffice for now.

The next section reads: "the consent of all the parts, the scope of the whole (which is to give all glory to God),"—a statement that testifies to the Bible's *uniformity* and *comprehensiveness*.

With regard to its *uniformity*, it can rightly be said that no contradiction exists in the Bible concerning its doctrine or central message. Consider the thousands of years over which the Scriptures were written—each book, letter, and poem composed in its respective time by different authors: kings, prophets, priests, farmers, shepherds, fishermen, a tax collector, a physician, and others. The *harmony* and *cohesion* found from Genesis to Revelation, from cover to cover, is a profound testament to the divine authorship of Scripture. No purely human endeavor could ever achieve such consistency.

To illustrate the improbability of such unity: imagine gathering ten individuals from the same neighborhood—of the same ethnicity, age, and interests—and asking each to write their opinion on a controversial subject. The likelihood that all ten responses would be in perfect agreement—100% harmonious—is so astronomically low that it would be deemed practically impossible. And yet, in the case of Scripture, we are dealing not with ten authors, but plus or minus forty; not with a few years, but millennia; not with shared backgrounds, but with vastly diverse circumstances. And yet, what do we find? Perfect doctrinal and theological *unity*. What more could we possibly require to appreciate the supernatural uniformity of the Word of God?

And to think—Holy Scripture is far more comprehensive than a mere treatment of a single subject. It addresses every aspect of human life, every function of mankind under the sun—if not directly, then indirectly. Scripture speaks to human rights, moral absolutes, faith, beauty, commerce, ethics, belief systems, historical events, the family, the institution of marriage, etc., and as it speaks to every aspect of man's function, it wholly reveals the will of God for mankind.

The next phrase in this fifth paragraph states:

> the full discovery it makes of the only way of man's salvation, and many other incomparable excellencies, and entire perfections thereof, are arguments whereby it does abundantly evidence itself to be the Word of God.

Put simply, the Word of God is the only source by which we may know the way of salvation. Apart from God's written revelation, all we could discern from creation is that we need redemption—that something is broken and requires restoration. The fallen state of our world makes that abundantly clear. Yet while general revelation testifies to our need for salvation, it does not and cannot reveal how we may be saved. This is precisely why God gave us His written Word—to reveal not only how we can be saved, but through Whom: Jesus Christ, the Son of God, who gave His life on the cross to pay the debt of our sin.

And indeed, there is much more that could be said about the many excellencies of the Word— each bearing witness to its divine origin and inspiration. Yet the *Confession* presents all of this in order to arrive at a culminating point:

> yet notwithstanding, our full persuasion and assurance of the infallible truth, and divine authority thereof, is from the inward work of the Holy Spirit bearing witness by and with the Word in our hearts.

The greatest evidence, the absolute and irrefutable evidence, that Holy Scripture is infallible truth and that it carries divine authority, is the *transformative change it produces in the human heart.*

When the Spirit of God touched our hearts of stone—hearts that were spiritually dead in trespasses—He made them hearts of living flesh, enabling us to receive the Word of God for what it truly is and to respond with willing obedience.

And now, having the Holy Spirit dwelling within us, we can testify, as Christians, that this Word is indeed from God, for it has produced a change within us, and continues to do so.

I often say that Holy Scripture is like a surgical knife—a tool wielded by the Spirit of God to correct all that has gone wrong within us, cutting away the cancer of sin that has corrupted our being.

All of this is powerfully conveyed in the fifth paragraph of the first chapter of the *Confession*, and the Scriptural references it provides in support are as follows:

The first is John 16:13-14, which says:

[13] When the Spirit of truth comes, he will guide you into all the truth, for he will not speak on his own authority, but whatever he hears he will speak, and he will declare to you the things that are to come. [14] He will glorify me, for he will take what is mine and declare it to you.

Here, Jesus is speaking to His disciples about the coming of the Holy Spirit—that when the Spirit is given (as He was on the Day of Pentecost, Acts 2), this third person of the Triune God would guide believers into all truth.

How does the Spirit do this? By means of the Word of God. The Spirit provides the necessary illumination to rightly understand and interpret the Scriptures.

And this same Spirit does not speak on His own authority, but communicates what is given by the Father and the Son. For the Spirit is not independent from the Father and the Son, but is one with them, forming the Triune Godhead.

The Spirit will exalt the Son, and will declare to us what has been revealed by Christ—which is precisely what we find communicated in the Word.

The next reference provided is 1 Corinthians 2:10-12, which says:

> [10] these things God has revealed to us through the Spirit. For the Spirit searches everything, even the depths of God. [11] For who knows a person's

thoughts except the spirit of that person, which is in him? So also no one comprehends the thoughts of God except the Spirit of God. [12] Now we have received not the spirit of the world, but the Spirit who is from God, that we might understand the things freely given us by God.

We will soon arrive at a section in our study of the *1689 Baptist Confession* where we will examine the doctrine of the Holy Spirit more fully. Thus, with respect to the present text, I will note only that the Holy Spirit is credited as knowing God exhaustively, precisely because the Spirit is one with God. There is nothing hidden between the Father, the Son, and the Holy Spirit.

The instances in the Gospels where Jesus states that the Father knows certain things which the Son does not (e.g., Matt. 24:36; Mark 13:32; Acts 1:7) are temporally constrained to His earthly ministry. During this period, the Son voluntarily refrained from accessing certain divine knowledge until His ascension to the Father.

The key point of the text, in relation to this part of the *Confession*, is this: the Spirit of God—the Holy Spirit—was given to God's people in order to reveal, illuminate, and grant understanding of what is freely given to us by God.

And what is that which has been "freely given" to us? According to the apostle Paul in his letter to the Corinthians, it is the written, inscripturated revelation of God. In order to rightly understand what comes from God, divine assistance is required, owing to the limitations imposed by our fallen nature. It is this Spirit of God who bears witness to the trustworthiness of Holy Scripture.

The final reference is 1 John 2:20 and verse 27, which says:

> [20] But you have been anointed by the Holy One, and you all have knowledge… [27] But the anointing that you received from him abides in you, and you have no need that anyone should teach you. But as his anointing teaches you about everything, and is true, and is no lie—just as it has taught you, abide in him.

85

According to the apostle John, the Holy Spirit anoints us, meaning that He empowers us for a particular task—namely, to live as the people of God. This same Spirit provides us with all knowledge. But how? By means of the study of Scripture.

Once again, it is the Spirit of God who enables us to understand the Word of God, so that we might attain the knowledge of God, insofar as it has been revealed to us.

As for verse 27, there has been some confusion regarding how best to interpret John's words, particularly due to a common misinterpretation—namely, that John is suggesting we do not need teachers. But if that were true, God would not have instituted the offices of pastor and teacher, nor would He have called the apostles—such as Peter, James, John, and Paul—to instruct the church. How then are we to interpret this verse? We cannot take it literalistically, as such a reading would contradict John's own intent in writing the epistle, which itself is an act of teaching and instruction. What John is affirming is that the Spirit of God, not man, is the ultimate authority. It is not man who reveals the truth, but God. It is not from man that truth originates, but from God, who reveals truth to man and communicates it through man. Accordingly, with reference to Holy Scripture, we understand that though Scripture was written by men, it originated in God, and therefore is authoritative and applicable to all people, across all ages, and among every tongue.

Undoubtedly, John is also alluding to that future day of consummation, when all things will be renewed. On that day, instruction will no longer be necessary, for the law of God will be written upon our hearts, and His will will be inherently known and obeyed by all. No more will we wrestle with the *noetic* effects of sin. We await that day with hope, but in the meantime, what we have now is sufficient: the Word of God, and the Holy Spirit who grants us the understanding we need.

As the *Confession* states:

Our full persuasion and assurance of the infallible truth and divine authority thereof, is from the inward work of the Holy Spirit bearing witness by and with the Word in our hearts.

THE HOLY SCRIPTURES
CH. I, PAR. 6

The whole counsel of God concerning all things necessary for His own glory, man's salvation, faith and life, is either expressly set down or necessarily contained in the Holy Scripture: unto which nothing at any time is to be added, whether by new revelation of the Spirit, or traditions of men.[9] Nevertheless, we acknowledge the inward illumination of the Spirit of God to be necessary for the saving understanding of such things as are revealed in the Word,[10] and that there are some circumstances concerning the worship of God, and government of the church, common to human actions and societies, which are to be ordered by the light of nature and Christian prudence, according to the general rules of the Word, which are always to be observed.[11]

[9] *2 Tim. 3:15-17; Gal. 1:8,9*
[10] *John 6:45; 1 Cor. 2:9-12*
[11] *1 Cor. 11:13,14; 1 Cor. 14:26,40*

THE FIRST SENTENCE of this paragraph provides an apt summary of all that precedes it in the opening chapter of the *1689 Baptist Confession*. It also serves as a fitting review for us, affirming that the "whole counsel of God"—encompassing the entirety of Scripture from Genesis to Revelation—reveals everything necessary concerning the glory of God, the salvation of mankind, the gift of faith, and living life *Coram Deo* (before the face of God).

If anything further concerning these matters is not revealed in Scripture, it is because such knowledge is not necessary for us to know. It is God alone who determines what knowledge is necessary, and what knowledge remains hidden.

For example, Scripture speaks clearly about the future bodily resurrection and the renewal of all things at the return of Christ (cf. Phil. 3:20–21; 1 Cor. 15:35–38; Rev. 21). Yet, comparatively little is revealed about the intermediate state—that period between the believer's physical death and the bodily resurrection.

We are told in Colossians 3:3, "...you have died, and your life is hidden with Christ in God." This verse holds a dual meaning. It first refers to our spiritual state—that we have died to sin and have been made alive in Christ. As Paul explains elsewhere, prior to our regeneration by the Holy Spirit, we were spiritually dead in our trespasses (Eph. 2:1–10). But the verse also refers to the interim state—that upon physical death, our lives are hidden with Christ. There is, without doubt, an element of mystery here. And if we are honest in our reading of Scripture, we must acknowledge that we are not given many details about this interim period.[1]

Yet what is revealed—however limited—is sufficient. What, then, is the point I am emphasizing? It is the doctrine of the *sufficiency of Scripture*. And it is God who determines what is sufficient—not man.

---

1. See Tim Mackey and Jon Collins, "Heaven & Earth", *Bible Project*. Accessed March 12, 2023, https://bibleproject.com/podcast/heaven-earth-revisited/.

Who are we to demand more? We are but dust. Mere creatures before the Creator. What can the clay demand of the potter? Do we have the right to claim more revelation than what He has given? Certainly not. As pastor and author Barry Cooper rightly states: "the Bible is sufficient, in itself, to tell us everything we must believe in order to be saved and what we must do in order to please God."[2]

Consider the fact that our first parents began with all the knowledge necessary for life and godliness. Yet, because they sought knowledge beyond what was necessary, they fell into sin (Gen. 3). This is not to suggest that Christians are prohibited from inquiring minds or from studying God's creation. On the contrary, there is good reason we can (and should) engage in disciplines such as the sciences. Being a Bible-believing Christian does not mean that we are opponents of "science," as the fallen world often caricatures us. It was, after all, the Dutch Christian philosopher Herman Dooyeweerd

2. Barry Cooper, "The Sufficiency of Scripture", *Ligonier.* Accessed July 16, 2023, https://www.ligonier.org/podcasts/simply-put/the-sufficiency-of-scripture/

(1894–1977) who developed and articulated a distinctly Christian philosophical and scientific enterprise, and he was widely recognized as The Netherlands' most original thinker. And by no means is he alone. Throughout the history of Western society, numerous Christian thinkers have made significant contributions to the development of the sciences. Thus, the issue is not science itself—nor is it what we study, or even whether we study—but rather, *why* we study.

Do we study the world around us to glorify God, submitting our inquiry to His Word revelation? Or do we study it in order to be like God, grasping at knowledge in a way that is inappropriate for a creature? This crucial distinction is seen between Christian scientists, who uphold the authority of Scripture, and unbelieving scientists, who elevate their own intellect and method as the final authority. That, however, is a discussion I have reserved for the doctrine of creation.

Returning to what God has deemed necessary for us to know, it must be stated that what *is* revealed in God's Word is not easily exhausted. What do I mean by this? I mean that not just anyone can become an expert theologian. While Holy Scripture is simple enough for us to grasp God's message, and we are all, in a general sense, theologians because we believe and profess doctrine, the Word of God is also incredibly and immeasurably profound, intricate, and complex. One could spend a lifetime studying the Word of God and still not exhaust its riches. Consider the entire history of the church since its inception in the New Testament: with each passing generation, we have delved deeper into the Word of God, attaining a clearer understanding of its meaning and application as it relates to all areas of life. However, such understanding does not come naturally.

There are several scholars in seminaries and universities who specialize in Biblical Studies but who do not uphold the authority of Scripture. These are often referred to as "liberal" scholars because, rather than affirming the truth and authority of Holy Scripture, they undermine it and seek to destroy

God's true church. Several prolific liberal scholars today, such as John Dominic Crossan and Bart Ehrman, are well-known. Many of their books are available at local bookstores like Chapters, Cole, or Indigo. Yet rather than provoking doubt or skepticism regarding the integrity of God's Word, the rise and influence of liberal scholarship actually serves to affirm the teaching of Scripture—specifically, that there will always be those who seek to distort the gospel and deceive the church. This will lead us to the next sentence in the *1689 Baptist Confession*. But before proceeding, consider one of the biblical references provided for this first sentence in paragraph six of chapter one: Galatians 1:8-9.

When the apostle Paul wrote to the church in Galatia in response to news that someone had added something foreign to the teaching of the gospel, he stated:

[8] But even if we or an angel from heaven should preach to you a gospel contrary to the one we preached to you, let him be accursed. [9] As we have said before, so now I say again: If anyone is preach-

ing to you a gospel contrary to the one you received, let him be accursed.

What is the context here? The Christian Galatians had been visited by the Judaizers—false teachers who claimed that Gentiles needed to become Jews and observe Jewish rituals (such as circumcision) in order to be saved and considered true Christians. In doing so, they were introducing a salvation by works, when the Galatian church had originally received a gospel of salvation by grace.

The point made by Paul is clear: anything contrary to the revelation of Scripture is to be rejected and treated as accursed. Nothing is to be added to biblical revelation, for it is complete and perfect in the sight and will of God.

Now, this is not to say that we cannot know things outside of Scripture—Scripture is not a general textbook that directly addresses every sphere of creation (e.g., business, science, academia, etc.). Rather, the point is that nothing outside of Scripture can be elevated to its place of authority. Nothing can be added to its finality. The Word alone, as the inspired Word of God, establishes the parameters from which we can rightly understand and engage with creation and culture. As John Calvin once put it, Holy Scripture is the "spectacles" through which we are enabled to see and understand the world.

Returning to the matter of comprehending Scripture, it should now be evident that possessing the highest intellectual capacity does not necessarily render Scripture more comprehensible in terms of its true meaning. The liberal scholars of past and present are clear evidence that academic accolades are insufficient for rightly understanding the Word of God.

If intellectual status alone were sufficient, then the Pharisees, scribes, and Sadducees would have understood the teachings of Jesus. But they did not. Why? Because something else is required—something only God can provide—that would cancel out the intellectual myopia caused by our sin.

Here is the first half of the second sentence:

Nevertheless, we acknowledge the inward illumination of the Spirit of God to be necessary for the saving understanding of such things as are revealed in the Word…

In other words, we need the Spirit of God—the Holy Spirit, the third person of the Trinity—to grant us *illumination*. The term *illumination* literally means to light up, to brighten, or to bring clarity. Merriam-Webster defines it as "the action of illuminating or state of being illuminated, such as spiritual or intellectual enlightenment."

In the context of the *1689 Baptist Confession*, and in accordance with how Christians understand the biblical doctrine of illumination, it refers to the Spirit-empowered process of perceiving spiritual truths—truths that suddenly make sense and move us toward life application. It is akin to the moment when a light bulb turns on in the mind upon reading a passage of Scripture, granting newfound understanding. Or the moment when an insight emerges that had previously escaped one's discernment. This can occur during personal Bible reading, in the hearing of a sermon, or in any setting where the Word of God is central. *Illumination* is both a spiritual and intellectual awakening, brought about by the indwelling Spirit of God as we engage with the divine revelation of Scripture.

Who, then, can receive this illumination? Only those who have been born again (John 3:3), those who have repented and believe in Jesus (Mark 1:15), those who have been adopted as children of God (Rom. 8:14–17). Salvation occurs once in a believer's life, but illumination may occur repeatedly and in varying degrees throughout the Christian life. Where do we find support for this in the Scriptures? The *1689 Baptist Confession* cites John 6:45, which states:

> [45] It is written in the Prophets, 'And they will all be taught by God.' Everyone who has heard and learned from the Father comes to me—

In this instance, Jesus explains to His followers that it is God who teaches His people. But does this mean we should not pursue academic study? Does it mean we should avoid enrolling in online Bible courses or attending seminary? Certainly not. Such a conclusion would be short-sighted and simplistic.

These tools—when used rightly and submitted to the authority of Scripture—can be greatly beneficial for our spiritual and intellectual growth. Rather, what Jesus means is that God alone is the true Revealer. It is God who serves as the chief interpreter, and God who is the ultimate Teacher. Whatever you may learn from a professor, pastor, or Bible teacher—they are not the source of the truth illuminated in your heart, but conduits through whom God speaks to our hearts. Just as it is the Holy Spirit who opens our eyes to the truth of the gospel, so too it is the Spirit who enlightens us to understand the rest of Scripture. Salvation is the result of the first illumination of the Spirit. Salvation is the result of the first instance of the Holy Spirit's illumination, and what follows are instances of our on-going sanctification.

The other biblical reference provided is 1 Corinthians 2:9-12, which states:

⁹ But, as it is written,

"What no eye has seen, nor ear heard,

nor the heart of man imagined,
what God has prepared for those who love him"—

[10] these things God has revealed to us through the Spirit. For the Spirit searches everything, even the depths of God. [11] For who knows a person's thoughts except the spirit of that person, which is in him? So also no one comprehends the thoughts of God except the Spirit of God. [12] Now we have received not the spirit of the world, but the Spirit who is from God, that we might understand the things freely given us by God.

Here is the apostle Paul, writing to the church in Corinth, explaining that it is the Spirit of God who grants us understanding. The gift of divine revelation must be accompanied by the Spirit in order for us to comprehend it—to open it, so to speak— for otherwise it remains closed to us and shrouded in mystery.

How is it that the Spirit of God is able to unveil our eyes to perceive the truth of God and not some other agent? It is because it is the Holy Spirit who searches the depths of God, who knows the mind of

God, and who thus reveals the truth of God. This is so because the Holy Spirit is *one* with the Father and the Son, being of the same divine *substance*. As Paul affirms, it is "God" who teaches us His Word.

What, then, follows in the rest of the second sentence of this portion of the *Confession*?

> ...and that there are some circumstances concerning the worship of God, and government of the church, common to human actions and societies, which are to be ordered by the light of nature and Christian prudence, according to the general rules of the Word, which are always to be observed.

As noted earlier, the *1689 Baptist Confession* acknowledges that Scripture does not address every specific detail—it is not intended as a manual for every academic or practical discipline. Nevertheless, it fulfills its divine purpose: to reveal God and His glory, to declare His redemptive plan for creation, and to instruct us in how we are to live before Him in faith.

As the Word of God, Scripture establishes the parameters by which we may understand how to act in a manner that is in accordance with God's will and subject to His revealed truth. Within these parameters, there is a measure of freedom to discern, for instance, what worship may look like, or how church governance is to be structured. This is not a license to do whatever we please, but a freedom to function within that which has already been revealed and established by the Word of God. What, then, might be an example?

At the end of each year, the church observes Advent as part of its corporate worship. On one particular occasion, a faithful Christian brother reached out to express his concern—not because he believed Advent to be a pagan observance (which he rightly denied), but because he was convinced that the church should not celebrate or observe it at all. His reasoning was grounded in adherence to the *regulative principle of worship*.

What is the regulative principle of worship? It is a doctrine upheld by some within the Reformed tradition, which holds that the church must worship God only in ways that are expressly commanded in Scripture, and that anything not positively prescribed is to be excluded from public worship. Those who subscribe to this principle would typically refrain from celebrating events such as Advent and Easter, avoid the use of certain instruments, and be particularly stringent regarding what is deemed permissible in the worship service. In simpler terms, the regulative principle seeks to order the church's worship exclusively according to what is explicitly commanded in Scripture, allowing for nothing beyond that.

In the case of the church I pastor, we do not hold to the regulative principle, and it appears that the *1689 Baptist Confession*—despite being a thoroughly Reformed document—does not fully endorse it either. Rather, both the *1689 Baptist Confession* and our practice reflect a commitment to what is known as the *normative principle of worship.* What is the normative principle? It teaches that any element or practice in public worship is permissible so long as it is not explicitly forbidden by Scripture. This principle allows for greater flexibility, such as the use of various musical instruments (piano, guitar, violin, cajón, etc.) and seasonal observances like Advent.

Does this mean we can disregard God's commands regarding how He is to be worshipped? Not at all. To do so would risk offering what Scripture describes as "strange fire." In Leviticus 10:1, the sons of Aaron deviated from God's specific instructions in worship, and when they presented unauthorized fire before the Lord, they were put to death. This account serves as a solemn reminder that God takes worship seriously.

Both principles, if misapplied, can result in error. On one side lies the danger of legalism—binding consciences where Scripture does not. On the other side lies the error of licentiousness—permitting what God has clearly forbidden. Both extremes undermine the purpose of the principles of worship and distort the holiness and reverence that should characterize our approach to God.

Regarding the debate between the *regulative* and *normative principles*, there is room for charitable disagreement amongst Christians. The church has engaged in a long-standing discussion regarding these two principles, and it is not necessary to delve further into that matter at this point. For now, it suffices to note that the *Confession* provides Scriptural support for the idea that certain circumstances of worship are to be governed by Christian prudence. One example is 1 Corinthians 11:13–14, where Paul addresses whether a woman should pray to God with her head uncovered, or whether it is disgraceful for a man to have long hair. This passage does not issue a universal prescription that wives must cover their heads or that men must wear their hair short. Rather, Paul is speaking to a culturally relevant concern among the Corinthians and exhorts them to judge for themselves what is proper within their context.

A further passage that brings greater clarity is 1 Corinthians 14:26 and 40, which reads:

[26] What then, brothers? When you come together, each one has a hymn, a lesson, a revelation, a tongue, or an interpretation. Let all things be done for building up… [40] But all things should be done decently and in order.

Note the balance presented in the text: there is freedom in worshipful expression—everything is permissible so long as it edifies—yet all things must be done decently and in order, in accordance with what God has commanded. We are to do what God commands, and at the same time, we are free to engage in whatever is not expressly prohibited by Him. This balance is essential for the church as it seeks to worship God faithfully and reverently in every aspect of life.

This portion of the *1689 Baptist Confession* therefore addresses not only corporate worship, but also how the church conducts itself in matters of governance and in its engagement with the world. How are such matters to be rightly determined? The phrase "by the light of nature" appears to refer to God's general revelation in creation; if so, then the Word of God must serve as the interpretive lens through which general revelation is rightly understood. That said, I find the phrase "Christian prudence" particularly compelling—it denotes the Spirit-wrought wisdom granted to believers. Ultimately, however, our final and supreme authority remains the Word of God, as the *1689 Baptist Confession* rightly states: "according to the general rules of the Word, which are always to be observed."

THE HOLY SCRIPTURES
CH. I, PAR. 7-8

All things in Scripture are not alike plain in themselves, nor alike clear unto all;[12] yet those things which are necessary to be known, believed and observed for salvation, are so clearly propounded and opened in some place of Scripture or other, that not only the learned, but the unlearned, in a due use of ordinary means, may attain to a sufficient understanding of them.[13]

[12]   *2 Pet. 3:16*
[13]   *Ps. 19:7; Psalm 119:130*

BEAR IN MIND WHAT WAS stated in the last paragraph concerning the need for the Spirit's illumination. While the basic message of Scripture can be grasped and communicated with clarity, not all portions of Scripture are equally easy to understand. Books such as Ecclesiastes, the Song of Solomon, and Revelation, along with several other texts, require trained instruction to be rightly read, interpreted, and understood.

Consider, for instance, what the apostle Peter writes concerning the writings of the apostle Paul:

> ...as [Paul] does in all his letters when he speaks in them of these matters. There are some things in them that are hard to understand, which the ignorant and unstable twist to their own destruction, as they do the other Scriptures (2 Peter 3:16).

What happens when we lack trained instruction in the Scriptures? As the apostle Peter warns, the ignorant and unstable twist the meaning of the texts to their own destruction—a warning we see tragically fulfilled today in the rise of false gospels and teachings such as the prosperity gospel, the word of faith movement, and various end-times conspiracies. Being trained in the Scriptures is essential not only for attaining a true understanding of God's Word but also for effectively refuting false doctrines and misinterpretations. This form of training is known as *hermeneutics*—a required course in most seminaries and an area that faithful local churches also strive to teach more informally.

What is *hermeneutics*? It is the study and methodology of biblical interpretation, concerned with uncovering the meaning and significance of the text. Such training is necessary because the Bible was not written in our contemporary context. It was composed thousands of years ago, by multiple authors, in diverse historical and cultural settings, and in different languages. However—and here we take great comfort—what God has revealed in His Word concerning our need for repentance and salvation is sufficiently clear for even the untrained reader to grasp.

To support this, the *Confession* cites Psalm 19:7, which declares:

> The law of the Lord is perfect,
>   reviving the soul;
> the testimony of the Lord is sure,
>   *making wise the simple*; (italicism mine)

As well as Psalm 119:130:

> The unfolding of your words gives light;
> *it imparts understanding to the simple.* (italicism mine)

In essence, Scripture is sufficiently clear to accomplish its divinely intended purpose: *to guide individuals to salvation and righteousness, through the illumination of the Spirit of God.* It is the Holy Spirit who brings about both spiritual and intellectual awakening, enabling the believer to grasp the meaning of the text—much like a light bulb illuminating within the mind.

This is what fundamentally distinguishes believers from unbelievers who study the Word of God: believers have received the true meaning of the text, while unbelievers remain unable to comprehend it. Their lack of understanding is not due to the meaning being hidden or obscure, but because they are spiritually dead in their sins and therefore spiritually blind. Those who come to saving faith through the Scriptures do so only because the Holy

Spirit first grants life and sight to those who were once dead and blind.

We now proceed to paragraph eight, which states:

> *The Old Testament in Hebrew (which was the native language of the people of God of old),[14] and the New Testament in Greek (which at the time of the writing of it was most generally known to the nations), being immediately inspired by God, and by His singular care and providence kept pure in all ages, are therefore authentic; so as in all controversies of religion, the church is finally to appeal to them.[15] But because these original tongues are not known to all the people of God, who have a right unto, and interest in the Scriptures, and are commanded in the fear of God to read,[16] and search them,[17] therefore they are to be translated into the vulgar language of every nation unto which they come,[18] that the Word of God dwelling plentifully in all, they may worship Him in an acceptable manner, and through patience and comfort of the Scriptures may have hope.[19]*

[14]   *Rom. 3:2*
[15]   *Isa. 8:20*
[16]   *Acts 15:15*
[17]   *John 5:39*
[18]   *1 Cor. 14:6,9,11-12,24,28*
[19]   *Col. 3:16*

This paragraph allows us to explore the preservation of Holy Scripture throughout history. Chronologically, we begin with the Old Testament, which was written primarily in ancient Hebrew. As the *1689 Baptist Confession* rightly states, this was the "native language of the people of God of old."

This is confirmed not only within the Old Testament texts themselves but also in the testimony of the apostle Paul, who writes in Romans 3:2:

> Much in every way. To begin with, the Jews were entrusted with the oracles of God.

Surprised to learn that Hebrew was not the only language used in the Hebrew Scriptures? Aramaic was also employed in select portions—most notably in parts of the Book of Daniel and the Book of Ezra.

How are we to understand the composition, transmission, and preservation of the Old Testament? At the outset, it must be acknowledged that from the events in the Garden of Eden to the exodus of the Hebrews from Egypt, there is no extant evidence of written records documenting these occurrences—at least none presently known to us. What did exist, however, is what biblical scholars refer to as the "oral tradition."

This term denotes the faithful transmission of historical narratives—such as the creation account, the fall of man, the dispersion at Babel, and the patriarchal histories—through oral recitation passed down across generations. In modern, text-centered cultures, oral transmission is frequently regarded with skepticism and often associated with unreliability. It is sometimes likened to the children's game "broken telephone," wherein a message becomes distorted as it moves from person to person.

Such assumptions, however, do not reflect the historical reality of oral-based societies in the Ancient Near East. In those cultures, oral tradition was considered both reliable and authoritative. These communities operated with an inherent system of *communal correction*: should a narrative be recited inaccurately, the broader community would identify the error and correct it, thereby preserving the integrity of the account across generations.

Consider, for example, how Muslims in the Middle East are able to memorize and recite the entire Qur'an without reference to the written text. If a passage is recited incorrectly, others are quick to correct the mistake. While Muslims may have begun with a written text, they developed an oral tradition rooted in that text. Although this differs from the oral tradition and culture of the Ancient Near East, it nonetheless provides a helpful analogy for understanding the nature and function of oral-based societies.

To cite a scholarly assessment of ancient oral traditions, the following explanation illustrates why the oral, and not the textual, was often preferred:

> Textuality provided no means for relationship or discussion between teachers and students. . . . Furthermore, reading a book might lead someone to think they had learned a body of material, but for them only to repeat what was written in a book was an illusion of knowledge. . . . Orality functions particularly well in communicating powerful messages to smaller groups of people. (Walton and Sandy, LWS, 103, 92)

This indicates that these ancient civilizations were not limited in their use of written texts due to a lack of advancement or education; rather, they possessed a distinct vision and preference for how information was to be communicated and preserved. Nevertheless, while the oral tradition proved sufficient for a time, it was not God's will for it to remain the primary mode of transmission.

As the knowledge of God's acts and words spread over larger territories and extended across longer periods, conflicting accounts would inevitably have arisen—creating an opportunity for Satan to corrupt the transmission of divine revelation. Thus, although oral traditions were indeed reliable and regarded as authoritative, they were not a viable long-term solution. This transition helps explain why the West today has become a predominantly *text-based* culture.

This emphasis on oral tradition is essential for understanding the background, nature, and integrity of the content of the Pentateuch—the first five books of the Old Testament. All historical events deemed significant by God, from creation to the exodus, were ultimately committed to writing by the prophet Moses, who, being inspired by the Spirit of God, converted what had been preserved orally into *inscripturated* revelation.

Before raising concerns about the possibility of omissions or inaccuracies, it is important to recall that Moses was uniquely privileged among the prophets—one who could speak with God face to face. Given his intimate fellowship with God—including the unparalleled experience of beholding God's glory—it is implausible to suggest that Moses would err in his recording of these events.

Moreover, having been inspired by the Spirit of God, Moses, like all the biblical authors, was preserved from error in his writing. One who is inspired by the Spirit cannot err in that which he has been divinely appointed to record.

From the composition of the Pentateuch onward, the remainder of the Old Testament was written, copied, and reproduced to ensure its preservation. To summarize the key points regarding the transmission and preservation of the Old Testament: evidence of private copying of its books does not emerge until the first century AD, during the time of Jesus. However, professional copyists (scribes) were employed by the Jewish community for the purpose of public worship. This practice gained greater prominence during the Babylonian exile, a period in which temple worship was replaced by the study of the Torah. Nevertheless, it is likely that the use of professional scribes and copyists predated the exile, indicating a longstanding tradition of textual preservation.

One of the rules that these copyists were required to follow was that the Torah was *not* to be copied from memory. The written Torah was to be transmitted in written form and therefore had to be copied from a written source. This rule rendered textual corruption in the transmission process virtually impossible. Furthermore, copyists were also required to read the Hebrew texts aloud as they transcribed them. If a mistake was made, the entire parchment or vellum had to be discarded.

Another significant fact worth considering is that the Old Testament is among the most accurately documented texts predating the life and ministry of Jesus Christ. We have access to thousands of manuscripts, with some fragments dating as far back as 600 BC. Notably, in the 1950s, the Dead Sea Scrolls were discovered in the Qumran caves of the Judaean Desert. These scrolls affirmed the accuracy of the Old Testament's transmission. Containing various books of the Old Testament in Hebrew, they were approximately one thousand years older than the manuscripts previously available.

During my seminary years, I conducted a study on the book of Isaiah and found that the text from the Dead Sea Scrolls was nearly identical to the Hebrew Bible we possess today. Biblical scholar Gleason Archer estimates a 95% accuracy rate, with the remaining 5% variance attributed to minor scribal errors and spelling differences, none of which affect the meaning of the text.[1] For those interested, the evidence for the faithful preservation and transmission of the Old Testament is readily accessible in museums, antiquity libraries, and online through digital scans. To further emphasize the historicity of the Old Testament, I have included a table that provides an overview of the available evidence. While not exhaustive, it offers a representative sample size.

It is important to clarify that our belief in the integrity of the Bible does not rest solely on external evidence. Rather, we believe in the Bible's integrity because it claims to be inspired by the Spirit of God, and we take God at His Word. Because we trust the

1.   See Gleason L. Archer, *A Survey of Old Testament Introduction*, revised and expanded ed. (Chicago, IL.: Moody Publishers, 2007).

121

Word of God, we anticipate that the facts of history and manuscript evidence will align with it.

Thus, the evidence does not function as proof of the Bible's truth but as an affirmation of what we already confess by faith. The ultimate authority for what is true rests with God Himself.

Here, then, is the table, drawn from the scholarly work of H. Wayne House and Joseph M. Holden:[2]

2.　H. Wayne House and Joseph M. Holden, *Charts of Apologetics and Christian Evidences* (Grand Rapids, MI.: Zondervan, 2006), chart. 43. Used by permission of Zondervan.

Name	Date	Earliest Copy or Copies	Biblical Books
Dead Sea Scrolls (DSS)	15th or 13th to 4th century BC	250 BC-AD 68	Includes 223-plus biblical manuscripts from every book of the Old Testament except Esther
DSS Isaiah Scroll A	8th century BC	150-100 BC	Complete copy of the book of Isaiah
DSS Habakkuk Commentary	7th century BC	64 BC	Portions of Habbakuk
Rylands Papyrus 458	15th or 13th century BC	150 BC	Contains Greek portions of Deut. 23-28
Nash Papyrus	15th or 13th century BC	150 BC-AD 68	Portion of the Decalogue (Exodus 20); Deut.(5:6-21); Shema (Deut. 6:4-9)

Peshitta	15th or 13th to 4th century BC	AD 100-200	Entire Old Testament in Syriac
Chester Beatty Papyri	15th or 13th to 8th century BC	AD 150	Large portions of Genesis, Numbers, Deuteronomy, Isaiah, Jeremiah, Daniel, Esther, and Ecclesiastes
Targum of Onkelos	15th or 13th century BC	AD 200	Torah
Codex Vaticanus (B)	15th or 13th century BC	AD 325	Entire Greek Old Testament and Apocrypha in uncials except portions of Genesis, 2 Kings, Psalms, 1 and 2 Maccabees, and the Prayer of Manasseh

Codex Ephraemi Rescriptus	13th-10th century BC	AD 345	Contains Job, Proverbs, Ecclesiastes, Song of Solomon
Codex Sinaiticus (aleph)	13th-14th centuries BC	AD 350	Half the Old Testament in Greek uncial
Latin Vulgate	15th or 13th to 4th century BC	AD 390-405	Entire Old Testament in Latin
Codex Alexandrinus (A)	15th or 13th to 4th century BC	AD 450	Entire Old Testament in Greek uncial
British Museum Oriental 4445	15th or 13th century BC	AD 850	Pentateuch
Codex Cairensis (C)	13th-4th centuries BC	AD 895	Former and Latter Prophets
Aleppo Codex	15th or 13th to 4th century BC	AD 900	Oldest complete Hebrew text of the Old Testament

Babylonian Codex of the Latter Prophets	7th-4th centuries BC	AD 916	Isaiah, Jeremiah, and the 12 Minor Prophets
Codex Leningradensis B19A (L)	15th or 13th to 4th century BC	AD 1008	Complete Hebrew text of the Old Testament
Samaritan Pentateuch (SP)	15th or 13th century BC	10th-11th century AD	Written in Samaritan characters

We now turn our attention to the New Testament. From the outset, it can be affirmed that the entirety of the New Testament was written within the first century AD. This means that its contents were written, collected, and copied during a time when eyewitnesses were still alive and could either confirm or challenge the events described. Had any inaccurate information regarding Jesus and His ministry been recorded, there would have been individuals present to object and safeguard the authentic account of what He did and said.

While we will not examine each letter of the New Testament in detail, here are the estimated dates of composition for the four Gospels:

It is believed that The Gospel of Matthew was written sometime between 60 and 80 AD. The Gospel of Mark, by contrast, is generally dated between 50 and 60 AD. The Gospel of Luke is likewise estimated to have been written between 60 and 80 AD, and The Gospel of John between 60 and 100 AD. Additionally, the Book of Acts, being the second volume of Luke's account, is included here and is typically dated between 62 and 64 AD. Notably, Acts concludes without reference to Paul's death under Emperor Nero, a significant omission that suggests it was written prior to that event.

Liberal scholars frequently dispute these early dates, preferring to assign later composition periods that place more distance between Jesus' ministry and the writing of the texts. This approach serves to support the theory that the gospel accounts evolved into myth over time. However, the textual evidence supports the claim that these writings were composed within the first century. A comparison between the New Testament documents and second-century writings reveals marked differences in names, literary style, and expressions. For example, when contrasted with the writings of the church fathers, the distinctiveness of New Testament Greek becomes apparent. Such evidence challenges the assumptions of liberal scholars, suggesting that their late dating of the New Testament is not grounded in the manuscript record but rather reflects preconceived ideological commitments.

Another argument often raised against the textual fidelity of the Gospels concerns the relationship among the Synoptic Gospels. It is commonly held that the Gospel of Mark was written first, followed by Matthew and Luke, both of which share substantial content with Mark. These three are referred to as the Synoptic Gospels because they include many of the same accounts, frequently presented in a similar sequence and with overlapping, or at times identical, wording. In contrast, the Gospel of John is largely distinct in both content and structure.

There is, in fact, nothing inherently problematic about this literary relationship. It is entirely plausible that Mark was written first, and that Matthew and Luke drew upon Mark as a source for their own Gospel compositions. Nevertheless, each Gospel possesses its own emphasis, theological focus, and stylistic approach, shaped by the author's intent and audience. Rather than undermining their reliability, these distinctions actually enhance the historical credibility of the Gospels.

Were all three Gospels entirely identical in wording and structure, it would resemble three witnesses in court offering verbatim testimony, raising concerns of collusion and thereby weakening the credibility of their accounts. Instead, what we find in the Synoptic Gospels are genuine, independent attestations of the life and ministry of Jesus Christ, each contributing uniquely and meaningfully to the broader narrative.

Returning to the *1689 Baptist Confession*, particularly the eighth paragraph of the first chapter, it affirms that the New Testament was originally written in Greek. This assertion is grounded in the fact that the earliest extant manuscripts are in ancient Greek, and because Greek functioned as the common language of the Roman Empire, second only to Latin. For the contents of the New Testament to be effectively disseminated to the churches throughout the known world, they necessarily had to be composed in the Greek language.

As the New Testament reached various people groups and cultures, it became necessary to translate its contents into other languages so that diverse populations might access and understand its teachings. As the *1689 Baptist Confession* states:

> But because these original tongues are not known to all the people of God, who have a right unto, and interest in the Scriptures, and are commanded in the fear of God to read, and search them, therefore they are to be translated into the vulgar language of every nation unto which they come...

This is why we have ancient manuscripts of the New Testament in a wide range of languages, including Armenian, Coptic, Gothic, Ethiopian, Old

Latin, Syriac, Georgian, Slavic, and many others.

To provide a sense of the volume of manuscript evidence available to us today, the following chart presents a representative sample:[3]

Language	Earliest MS (old)	Earliest MS (new)	Number of MSS (old)	Number of MSS (new)
Armenian	AD 887	AD 862	2000+	2000+
Coptic	Late 3rd c. AD	Late 3rd c. AD	Around 975	Around 975
Gothic	5th or 6th c. AD	5th or 6th c. AD	6	6
Ethiopian	10th c. AD	6th c. AD	600+	600+
Old Latin	4th c. AD	4th c. AD	50	110
Vulgate	4th c. AD	4th c. AD	10,000+	10,000+
Syriac	5th c. AD	Late 4th or Early 5th c. AD	350+	350+

3. Table drawn from Joseph M. Holden and Norman Geisler, *The Popular Handbook of Archaeology and the Bible: Discovering That Confirm the Reliability of Scripture* (Eugene, OR.: Harvest House Publishers, 2013).

Georgian	Late 9th c. AD	5th c. AD	43+	89
Slavic	10th c. AD	10th c. AD	4,000+	4,000+
Total Non-Greek Manuscripts				**18,130+**
Greek	AD 130 (or earlier)	AD 130 (or earlier)	5,838	5,856
Total Greek & Non-Greek Manuscripts				**23,986**

Naturally, challenges arise when translating texts into other languages. Even today, certain English expressions do not translate precisely into French, Spanish, or other languages, and vice versa. Nonetheless, it remains possible to communicate the central message in another language by employing different words or phrases that, while not identical, convey the intended meaning.

Skeptics often argue that the biblical text could have been altered or corrupted during the processes of copying or translation. In theory, this could be done with relative ease. This is precisely why the abundance of manuscripts is so valuable—it enables scholars to identify and assess textual variants.

To illustrate: imagine purchasing a large dictionary and attempting to alter the definition of a word. If you were to remove the ink and write in your own version, the alteration would quickly become apparent when compared with other copies in circulation. If only one dictionary reflects the change, while the rest remain consistent, the variant can be readily dismissed. This same principle applies to the ancient biblical manuscripts. The vast number of available copies allows scholars to compare texts, identify discrepancies, and thus ensure the reliability and integrity of the original text.

It is essential to understand how Scripture came to be—not to generate faith, but to strengthen our faith in what the Word of God teaches. The Bible we possess today is the inspired Word of God, and we affirm its inerrancy and infallibility. Does this mean that our English, Spanish, or other language translations are themselves inerrant and infallible? In one sense, yes, and in another, no.

Yes—insofar as they faithfully convey the written Word of God as it was originally given in Hebrew, Aramaic, and Greek. The original manuscripts (the *autographa*) are themselves inerrant and infallible. However, no—insofar as the modern translations are not, in and of themselves, inspired or free from all possible error. This is why, in the study of Scripture, it is crucial to consult the original languages in order to ensure accuracy in interpretation and meaning. The Word, as originally written, was inspired; subsequent translations, while necessary, are not inspired in the same manner.

Nevertheless, the translation of Scripture was indispensable, as Paul writes in 1 Corinthians 14:11: "If I do not know the meaning of the language, I will be a foreigner to the speaker and the speaker a foreigner to me." The translation of the Scriptures was vital for the proclamation of the gospel, enabling the advancement of God's kingdom to all nations.

On the matter of translation, the *1689 Baptist Confession* provides biblical justification. In Acts 15:15–18, Luke translates the Hebrew text of the prophet Isaiah into Greek. While this may go unnoticed in our English Bibles, it establishes a clear biblical precedent for translation. This is important in contrast to claims—such as those made by Muslims—that a holy text cannot be translated without losing its power or becoming corrupt. The Bible, by contrast, validates translation as a necessary and faithful means for the Word of God to reach every nation and tongue.

In 1 Corinthians 14:6, the apostle Paul writes:

> Now, brothers, if I come to you speaking in tongues, how will I benefit you unless I bring you some revelation or knowledge or prophecy or teaching?

In this context, Paul is referencing the gift of speaking in tongues (other languages), and he is saying, if I speak in tongues that you *do not* understand, how does that benefit you? They would be meaningless words to you. He clarifies this in verse 9:

> So with yourselves, if with your tongue you utter speech that is not intelligible, how will anyone know what is said? For you will be speaking into the air.

The same principle is provided in verses 11-12, which I had previously cited:

> [11] …but if I do not know the meaning of the language, I will be a foreigner to the speaker and the speaker a foreigner to me. [12] So with yourselves, since you are eager for manifestations of the Spirit, strive to excel in building up the church.

A brief comment on verse 12: It is noteworthy that Paul addresses this particular concern, as it remains highly relevant for many Christians today. He observes that believers are "eager for manifestations of the Spirit," which may include such expressions as speaking in tongues, miraculous signs, and other visible demonstrations of spiritual power. Yet, what is Paul's response? He exhorts them rather to "strive to excel in building up the church."

This distinction is striking. In our own time, many continue to pursue signs and wonders, while comparatively few devote themselves to the edification of the church. The apostle's words call for careful self-reflection. Which of the two describes you?

Returning to the matter of the translation of the Word of God, let us fast forward from the first century AD to the sixteenth century. By that time, the Roman Catholic Church had declared the Vulgate—a Latin translation of the Bible completed by St. Jerome between AD 383 and 404—to be the definitive and sole authoritative translation of Scripture. This, however, posed several problems.

First, the Church had no biblical authority to declare the Vulgate as the only legitimate version of Scripture. Second, the Latin text was accessible only to those who had received formal education in the Church—primarily monks and priests—or to those who already knew Latin, which, by the sixteenth century, represented a small minority of the population. The vast majority of people were therefore unable to read or understand the Bible, rendering God's Word effectively inaccessible to the common person.

This withholding of Scripture allowed for the perpetuation of ecclesiastical abuses, as the people were kept in ignorance of the truth. It was an act of spiritual cruelty that enabled the Papal institution to govern unchallenged. In response to this, the Reformer William Tyndale famously declared:

> I defy the Pope and all his laws; if God spares my life, I will cause a young farm boy to know more of the Scriptures than you do.[4]

Tyndale went on to translate the Bible into English, drawing upon the resources available to him from previous attempts to publish the English Scriptures. A parallel account can be found in Spain, where a former monk who had embraced Protestant convictions devoted his life to producing the first complete Spanish translation of the Bible. His name was Casiodoro de Reina, and he built upon earlier translation efforts to produce what is now known as *La Biblia del Oso*. Following its publication, Reina's mentee, Cipriano de Valera, undertook a careful revision and refinement of the

---

4.   "William Tyndale, God's Outlaw", *Christianity.com*.
       Accessed July 17, 2024, https://www.christianity.com/church/
       church-history/church-history-for-kids/william-tyndale-gods-
       outlaw-11634865.html/.

translation, resulting in the edition known as *La Biblia del Cántaro.* The labor of these men—conducted in exile, outside of Spain, while evading the reach of the Spanish Inquisition—culminated in the creation of the Reina-Valera Bible. This foundational translation for the Spanish-speaking church was born out of a deep desire to see the Word of God proclaimed clearly and faithfully in the Spanish language.

In the end, we may ask: What is the purpose of translating God's Word into our modern tongue? The *1689 Baptist Confession* articulates this clearly, as we have already seen, but to further answer this question, we turn to the passage it cites: Colossians 3:16.

> Let the word of Christ dwell in you richly, teaching and admonishing one another in all wisdom, singing psalms and hymns and spiritual songs, with thankfulness in your hearts to God.

Let that, then, be the reason why you should read Scripture daily—as exhorted in Colossians 3:16, and further supported by 2 Timothy 3:16–17.

All Scripture is breathed out by God and profitable for teaching, for reproof, for correction, and for training in righteousness, that the man of God may be complete, equipped for every good work.

THE HOLY SCRIPTURES
CH. 1, PAR. 9-10

The infallible rule of interpretation of Scripture is the Scripture itself; and therefore when there is a question about the true and full sense of any Scripture (which are not many, but one), it must be searched by other places that speak more clearly.[20]

[20] *2 Pet. 1:20–21; Acts 15:15–16*

THE NINTH PARAGRAPH of the first chapter of the *1689 Baptist Confession of Faith* affirms that the ultimate authority for interpreting Scripture is not man, but Scripture itself. Contrary to the claims held by many within Roman Catholicism, the pope is not the final interpretive authority. Nor are church councils, creeds, Reformers, Puritans, pastors, or elders. The inspired Word of God stands as its own authority, and all others are called to submit to it. The *1689 Baptist Confession*, by its own admission, is likewise subject to the authority of Scripture.

Furthermore, this paragraph affirms that when a passage of Scripture appears unclear or difficult to interpret, we are to turn to other portions of Scripture where the same doctrine or theme is treated with greater clarity. This principle not only upholds the sufficiency and authority of Scripture but also guards us against speculative interpretations in areas where Scripture has already spoken.

No one is exempt from this principle; it applies equally to *all*. That means that I myself must submit to the authority of the Word, and all that I write and teach must be measured against it. It is common for readers to approach Scripture with their own assumptions and personal experiences, whether positive or negative, which can inevitably shape their reading of the text. This is understandable, as we are all in the process of being redeemed and renewed.

Nevertheless, each time we engage with the Scriptures, we are called to set aside our presuppositions, diligently study the text, and seek to discern the original meaning intended by the Spirit of God. There is, in one sense, the intent of the human author, who wrote within a specific historical and cultural context, and in another sense, the intent of the Holy Spirit, who inspired the author to communicate divine truth.

Even where a text may contain both literal and spiritual elements, there remains only one central meaning. The *1689 Baptist Confession* affirms that there cannot be multiple, contradictory meanings to a single passage; rather, there is one true, unified meaning—that which is communicated by the Spirit of God.

What biblical references does the *1689 Baptist Confession* provide in support of this first principle? Consider, first, 2 Peter 1:20–21, which states:

> [20] knowing this first of all, that no prophecy of Scripture comes from someone's own interpretation. [21] For no prophecy was ever produced by the

will of man, but men spoke from God as they were carried along by the Holy Spirit.

In relation to what the apostle Peter writes here, some have raised doubts about the authority of the Word on the grounds that it was written by men. However, such skepticism would persist even if the Word had been delivered by an angel or inscribed on a gold tablet, as is claimed by the Mormons regarding their sacred text. God, in His wisdom, chose to communicate His Word through men in written form—a method more credible to us precisely because His revelation is not detached from historical reality but is instead embedded within it.

By contrast, certain religious traditions, such as Islam and Mormonism, assert that revelation comes from beyond their metaphysical and existential context. What they fail to recognize is that such a mode of revelation renders the message abstract and ultimately unintelligible to the human mind. The God who reveals Himself in Scripture is not disconnected from our world; He is not the god of Islam or Mormonism. Rather, the God of the Bible is deeply engaged with our reality, to the extent that He sent His Son, Jesus Christ, into our fallen world to accomplish its redemption.

How else, then, could the Scriptures have been written except through the hands of men, as God ordained? Yet, this does not mean that the Scriptures are the product of human speculation or private interpretation. In stark contrast to Charles Darwin—who, after visiting the Galapagos Islands, formulated his own interpretation of biological origins—the apostle Peter makes clear that no prophecy of Scripture originates from man's own interpretation. What was written came from the mind of God, though it was men who penned it. Such is the character of the Word of God.

The other biblical reference is Acts 15:15-16, which states:

> [15] And with this the words of the prophets agree, just as it is written, [16] "After this I will return, and I will rebuild the tent of David that has fallen; I will rebuild its ruins, and I will restore it."

This passage, taken from James's speech at the Jerusalem Council, complements what the apostle Peter wrote: that what was written was not of man's own interpretation, but rather God's inspired revelation. Mankind can say whatever he wants concerning the future, but that does not mean what he says will come to pass. The prophecies of the Old Testament are so precise and detailed that their fulfillment cannot be attributed to man. James noted that the prophets, despite living and ministering at different times, were in agreement in their prophecies. He refers in Acts 15:15–16 to the restoration of the kingdom of God, as God had promised David an everlasting dynasty—that although David's kingdom had fallen to ruins under the feet of the Gentiles, prophecy foretold that God would come to rebuild and restore it. This was fulfilled in Jesus, who came not only as God but also in the form of a man from the royal line of David. James not only affirms the divine nature of the Scriptures as having been inspired—that is, breathed out by God, meaning it originated from God—but also provides a clear interpretation of the Old Testament prophecies concerning a future kingdom: prophecies that were unclear at the time for the Jews, and that we would not understand unless we first had an understanding of the New Testament.

To summarize, paragraph 9 of the first chapter articulates two principles: (1) that Scripture is its own authority for its interpretation; and (2) that clearer passages are to be used to illuminate and interpret those that are less clear. These may rightly be referred to as *hermeneutical* principles, as they pertain to the interpretation of the Word.

Turning to paragraph 10 of the *1689 Baptist Confession*, it states:

> *The supreme judge, by which all controversies of religion are to be determined, and all decrees of councils, opinions of ancient writers, doctrines of men, and private spirits, are to be examined, and in whose sentence we are to rest, can be no other but the Holy Scripture delivered by the Spirit, into which Scripture so delivered, our faith is finally resolved.*[21]

[21]   *Matt. 22:29, 31, 32; Eph. 2:20; Acts 28:23*

Most of what is expressed in this final paragraph has already been addressed; however, a few additional points remain to be noted. While it is true that Scripture is its own authority, and that, whenever disagreements arise among us concerning our professed faith, we are to appeal to Scripture as the final authority, this principle also extends to religion more *broadly*. What do I mean by that? I meant that Scripture remains the ultimate authority in *all* matters pertaining to faith and practice.

To clarify: *religion*, in its proper sense, refers to *worship*—the outward expression of our heart's faith commitment. As a Christian people, we are *religious* in that we worship God; our *religion* is the manifestation of our biblical faith commitment. Yet, as is well known, there exists a distinction between *true religion* and *false religion*. True religion is the worship of the one true God as revealed in Scripture; false religion is the worship of anyone or anything within the created order. Another term used for false religion is "apostasy," denoting a falling away from the truth.

If ever a dispute arises regarding how we are to worship, whom we are to worship, or where we are to worship—and we must remember that worship encompasses all of life—then Scripture alone is to serve as the final authority. This implies that true worship accords with what Scripture reveals, while false worship deviates from it.

This concluding portion of the first chapter of the *1689 Baptist Confession*, which summarizes our doctrinal commitments, affirms the absolute truth of Scripture as God's inspired Word, and therefore, as inerrant (incapable of being wrong) and infallible (incapable of error).

It is important to provide some clarity as we consider disagreements both within and outside the church. Within the church, disagreements often arise over secondary issues, typically concerning the interpretation of less clear passages. This explains, in part, the existence of various denominations. Nevertheless, given the clarity and simplicity of Scripture's central message, there must be unity concerning the primary doctrines of the faith.

149

Can believers coexist and fellowship while holding differing views on secondary matters—such as eschatology, the exercise of spiritual gifts, or the expression of worship within church services? Yes, they can—and indeed, they should—provided the love of Christ is present and there is grace extended toward one another. Ultimately, what is now partially understood will be made fully known when we are face to face with Christ. In His presence, such secondary disagreements will fade into insignificance.

However, when it comes to disagreements between true and false religion—between the faith commitments of God's people and those who reject Him—there can be no agreement or "fellowship" with respect to creed. Can we coexist? Practically speaking, yes—we live side by side with unbelieving neighbors. But at the worldview level, there will inevitably be conflict. Scripture will remain our final authority, while the world will continue to oppose the truths revealed in it. Thus, while coexistence is possible in a civic and social sense, fellowship is not. There can be no fellowship between truth and error, between light and darkness. The distinction becomes evident.

This is why Jesus says to the unbelieving Sadducees in Matthew 22:29, "You are wrong, because you know neither the Scriptures nor the power of God." And to what was He referring? Jesus was addressing the Sadducees' mistaken belief that the resurrection of the dead is not taught in Scripture. This is why He responds:

> "And as for the resurrection of the dead, have you not read what was said to you by God: 'I am the God of Abraham, and the God of Isaac, and the God of Jacob?' He is not God of the dead, but of the living" (vv. 31-32).

Scripture is to be our ultimate authority because it alone provides *the authoritative interpretation of our created reality.* To reject the Scriptures, or to regard them as anything less than what they truly are, is to undermine the very foundation of the church. As Paul writes in Ephesians 2:20, the church is "built on the foundation of the apostles and prophets, Christ Jesus himself being the cornerstone."

Do you know how we came to be called "Christians"? The term was originally intended as a derogatory label by unbelievers, yet it became a title we now hold dear. It identifies us as followers of Christ. Likewise, in the seventh century, Muslims began referring to Christians by another name: "People of the Book." This, too, is a title we ought to embrace, for the Book—the Word of God—is our ultimate authority in all matters of life and thought. We ought to thank God for such a priceless treasure, though too often we take it for granted.

As we conclude the first chapter of the *1689 Baptist Confession*, consider this: can the same be said of us? Are we truly "People of the Book"? If not, we most certainly ought to be.

SCRIPTURE INDEX

Revelation

ABOUT THE CÁNTARO INSTITUTE
Inheriting, Informing, Inspiring

The Cántaro Institute is a reformed evangelical organization committed to the advancement of the Christian worldview for the reformation and renewal of the church and culture.

We believe that as the Christian church returns to the fount of Scripture as her ultimate authority for all knowing and living, and wisely applies God's truth to every aspect of life, her missiological activity will result in not only the renewal of the human person but also the reformation of culture, an inevitable result when the true scope and nature of the gospel is made known and applied.

www.ingramcontent.com/pod-product-compliance
Lightning Source LLC
Chambersburg PA
CBHW051312120626
46547CB00015B/2204